Praise

Come Along

"A gifted writer. The light of Scripture shines again through the prism of beauty and story."

—JOHN ORTBERG, best-selling author of *If You Want To Walk on Water You Have To Get Out of the Boat* and *When the Game Is Over, It All Goes Back in the Box*

"Jane Rubietta's books are as compelling as her platform presentations. She crafts her content with well-chosen word pictures and profound depth that beckons the readers to 'come along' as she leads them into a vibrant and transcendent relationship with Jesus. This book will deepen your faith."

—CAROL KENT, speaker and author of *A New Kind of Normal*

"Another powerful read on encounters with Jesus, self, those we love, and those we are trying to like. Jane addresses hope, healing, attitudes, needs, and longings with grace, grit, and God-centered wisdom. Each chapter ends with challenges and tools that are highly effective in helping us achieve deeper levels of intimacy. *Come Along* invites us to take the Lord's hand and walk through life with courage, anticipation, and zeal."

—ELLIE LOFARO, coauthor of *Spaghetti for the Soul* and author of *Leap of Faith*

"*Come Along* made me face the question, 'Am I following a set of phony rules and expectations in my attempts to be a "nice" Christian, or am I becoming the woman God imagined me to be?' With exquisite writing, Jane takes my real, everyday life in the twenty-first century and shows me how Jesus is relevant and present in every moment. Her unshakeable conviction in God's goodness and love convinced me to throw out my misguided attempts to be 'nice' and engage in an authentic relationship with Christ. 'When a woman encounters Jesus, she is changed,' Jane insists—and I was."

—LYNN AUSTIN, four-time Christy Award winner
and author of *Until We Reach Home*

"How does Jane Rubietta know me so well? Her refreshing honesty in *Come Along* promises to help you get in tune with who you are on the inside, and who God is in your life. She helps us slow down enough to reflect, draw closer, and journey into a more intimate faith experience with the God who loves us more than we can ever imagine."

—JILL SAVAGE, founder of Hearts at Home and author
of *Real Moms...Real Jesus*

"Jane Rubietta has done it again! Every time I read her books, I come away challenged, comforted, and encouraged to stop, wait, listen, and come closer to Jesus. I am a better person after reading the words of wisdom in *Come Along*."

—PAM FARREL, author of more than twenty-five books,
including the best-selling *Men Are like Waffles, Women
Are like Spaghetti* and *The Ten Best Decisions a Woman
Can Make*

come
along

Also by Jane Rubietta:

10 Illuminating Encounters with Jesus

come
along

The Journey
Into a
More Intimate Faith

Jane
Rubietta
author of *Come Closer*

WATERBROOK
PRESS

COME ALONG
PUBLISHED BY WATERBROOK PRESS
12265 Oracle Boulevard, Suite 200
Colorado Springs, Colorado 80921
A division of Random House Inc.

All Scripture quotations, unless otherwise indicated, are taken from the Holy Bible, New International Version®. NIV®. Copyright © 1973, 1978, 1984 by International Bible Society. Used by permission of Zondervan Publishing House. All rights reserved. Scripture quotations marked (NASB) are taken from the New American Standard Bible®. © Copyright The Lockman Foundation 1960, 1962, 1963, 1968, 1971, 1972, 1973, 1975, 1977. Used by permission. (www.Lockman.org). Scripture quotations marked (NKJV) are taken from the New King James Version®. Copyright © 1982 by Thomas Nelson Inc. Used by permission. All rights reserved. Scripture quotations marked (NLT) are taken from the Holy Bible, New Living Translation, copyright © 1996, 2004. Used by permission of Tyndale House Publishers Inc., Wheaton, Illinois 60189. All rights reserved.

Details in some anecdotes and stories have been changed to protect the identities of the persons involved.

ISBN 978-1-4000-7352-8

Published in association with the literary agency of Alive Communications Inc., 7680 Goddard Street, Suite 200, Colorado Springs, CO 80920, www.alivecommunications.com.

Published in the United States by WaterBrook Multnomah, an imprint of The Doubleday Publishing Group, a division of Random House Inc., New York.

WATERBROOK and its deer colophon are registered trademarks of Random House Inc.

Library of Congress Cataloging-in-Publication Data
Rubietta, Jane.
    Come along : the journey into a more intimate faith : 10 illuminating encounters with Jesus / Jane Rubietta.—1st ed.
        p. cm.
    Includes bibliographical references (p.   ).
    ISBN 978-1-4000-7352-8
    1. Christian women—Religious life. 2. Jesus Christ—Person and offices. I. Title.
    BV4527.R79 2008
    248.8'43—dc22

                                    2008034595

Printed in the United States of America
2008—First Edition

10 9 8 7 6 5 4 3 2 1

SPECIAL SALES
Most WaterBrook Multnomah books are available in special quantity discounts when purchased in bulk by corporations, organizations, and special-interest groups. Custom imprinting or excerpting can also be done to fit special needs. For information, please e-mail SpecialMarkets@WaterBrookMultnomah.com or call 1-800-603-7051.

• • • • •

For Ruthie
The most radiant woman I know

Ten Encounters with Jesus

The Illuminating Passages

Matthew 3:17: "This is my Son, whom I love; with him I am well pleased."

John 8:10–11: "Has no one condemned you?... Then neither do I condemn you," Jesus declared. "Go now and leave your life of sin."

Mark 10:51: "What do you want me to do for you?" Jesus asked.

Luke 18:7: "Will not God bring about justice for his chosen ones, who cry out to him day and night?"

Mark 5:34: "Daughter.... Go in peace and be freed from your suffering."

Luke 7:48: "Your sins are forgiven."

Luke 12:27 (NASB): "Consider the lilies, how they grow."

Luke 13:16: "Should not this woman...be set free on the Sabbath day?"

Matthew 15:11: "What goes into a man's mouth does not make him 'unclean,' but what comes out of his mouth, that is what makes him 'unclean.'"

Matthew 28:9–10: "Greetings.... Do not be afraid."

Contents

Introduction

Something was out of sync. I was getting more in touch with Jesus, knowing his heart, loving him more, feeling the energy that comes from staying close to him. I felt alive and bouncy and bright, like an Easter dress.

But along came work. And more work. And family stuff. And I started shortchanging my sleep, fretting a bit more. Grumpiness appeared. Or at any rate, the smiles disappeared. I felt like an old penny, its shine long destroyed. I started to look like the man on the penny too. (No, just kidding. I don't have a beard. Yet.)

And then my birthday rolled around. I hate it when my birthday comes and I'm feeling poor and cheap and sorry for myself, because then I don't want anyone to buy me anything. But this year, I wanted to really mean it when I said to friends and family, "You are my birthday gift, the very best gift possible."

I do mean that…but I also like toys: a sparkly top, a pair of glitzy earrings, perfume, dark chocolate. Girl stuff.

The heat index was stupidly high for June, and we decided to have my little birthday gathering in the only air-conditioned room in the house, our former garage. Believing to some extent in the motto "Fake it until you make it," I mustered up some pseudo good attitude, hauled tables and chairs, carried the silver and plates and glasses and pitchers of water and all the other accoutrements for a celebration meal down the stairs. I swatted mosquitoes and snipped flowers for low arrangements from our straggly, struggling gardens, then, as this was a combo birthday–Father's Day celebration, ran upstairs to wrap a few presents for the two fathers in the crowd.

Flopping onto the floor, with my legs spread out, I boxed the gifts. My mood sank lower than my knees, and I wanted to bawl. Hormones? Maybe. Lack of sleep? Maybe. Deadlines? Maybe. Problems with my soul? Definitely.

No wonder my soul was in trouble. In order to make it through the days, and nights, I had shifted gears into autopilot and ceased to truly encounter Jesus. Not only had I forgotten how to come closer to Jesus, the results showed on my face. I had stopped shining.

I'd begun to resemble the Grim Reaper in daily life.

And that afternoon, as I sat on the floor, needing to wrap gifts though I had kindly ordered everyone not to give *me* any presents, my heart felt crumbly, like old newspapers in the attic or last month's bread.

I shifted to my knees, put my face on the floor, and cried, "God, I do not want to live a lie. God, I want to be radiant with your love, I want others to see your light shining out of me, like I swallowed sunshine." And then, "Come alongside me, Jesus. Help me to encounter you, daily, minute by minute. I cannot live this life without your presence."

finding rays of hope every day

It seems so obvious: if the Christian life isn't about encountering Christ more deeply, we're getting the wrong message. So why do we make the Christian life so complicated, trying to fill in the chasm between hope and actuality with a new, improved Bible, or Bible study, or Scripture-reading plan, or method of prayer? We don't need a new Scripture software program for our computer. We don't need a new memory plan. We don't need to know the original language. Don't misunderstand: these are all good things. But what we really need, deep down, is to tuck in alongside Jesus. He simply holds out a hand and says, "Come along. Come with me on another adventure. Let me come along with you! Hold on to me, learn from me. My yoke is gentle, my burden light."

As we experience Christ more fully throughout the day, the results show on our faces. We are transformed from "glory to glory," as the Scriptures say (2 Corinthians 3:18, NASB).

Come Along is an invitation into that glory—a free, fuller, more intimate relationship with Jesus. It's about how, after that birthday, as I've held more tightly to Christ's hand and chosen to look for him in relationships and situations, troubles and joys— I feel different. Lighter. Brighter. I smile more. Carry less. Oh, I still battle thundercloud face, still wrestle with the darkness, with lack of joy. But since last summer, I began to dig into New Testament stories of Jesus and meet him in a brand-new way. These are some delightful interactions with Jesus as I've never known him before.

Come along with me and see. Let him take your hand and walk you through the hills and sands of Israel, down crowded streets and into interactions that will make your heart sing.

Along the way, you'll recognize a deep desire to be safe. And deeper even than that is the deepest of all longings: the longing for a love that will never leave us, for a Lover who will love us perfectly. We find that love in Jesus, only in Jesus, and when we are loved, safe, we are changed. We become more lovely.

As for that hot birthday in June—never have I enjoyed a party more. I felt like a candle. My flame may flicker, but God keeps stoking the fire, keeps me burning, brighter, every day.

how to come along

I want you to have that same kind of vibrant encounter with Jesus. Come along with me and you'll see that every chapter in this book begins with an illuminating quote about the encounter ahead. Mull over that quote, listen to it, ask yourself how it applies to you and your soul and the way you live. Then keep those questions at the front of your heart throughout the whole book. Because these encounters with Jesus are not so that you will learn more about him (although that is wonderful, and I hope that you do!) or learn more Scripture (although, of course, yes, please, Lord, help us learn more of your Word!). Rather, these encounters are intended to change us, to move us from one place to another. So when you come to Jesus's words at the top of each chapter, wait with those words; listen and really hear them.

Moving into the text of the chapter, into the encounter with Jesus, put yourself in the place of the people in the story. Go to the river, the temple, the party, the synagogue. With whom in the stories do you most identify? Perhaps keep a journal of your own encounters with Jesus as you join him in these various places.

Make the book your own as well: don't save it for someone else. Where do you doubt, question, hope? Where do tears come, longings press forward? Mark those things in the margins of this book so you can track your journey.

At the end of each chapter waits the friend you long for, the person who will ask you hard questions, invite you into silence, share Scripture for your meditation, challenge you with vulnerable prayers and ultimate application: how will you come alongside Jesus today, in what way?

This spiritual Companion shows up in these sections, inviting you to come along to:

transfer from dark to light

God's Word tells us that he has transferred us out of darkness and into light—and this section is a prayer place, a time for repentance, for confessing where you messed up, missed the point, made a spectacle. It's also a place, in that position of humility, of waiting for forgiveness. Be still here. There's no need to rush through the offered prayer. Wait a little longer until your own words form after praying through the written words of repentance.

transfix upon Christ

Still in silence, wait peacefully in the presence of Christ. If words start to get in your way, invite your worried heart to rest—*shhh*. Be still and calm. Maybe your silence will last only seconds or a minute or two. But cease-fire your own words, and just point your heart at God. Love God, and let God love you. Gaze at Jesus in stillness, as you used to adore your very first boyfriend, maybe; let Jesus love you back.

translate the meaning

These questions dive down to the meaning beneath our behaviors, beliefs, and attitudes. They invite us into honesty and into growth as we put ourselves into the encounters with Jesus and learn how to live differently as a result.

transform by renewing your mind

Romans 12:2 invites us to "be transformed by the renewing of [our] mind," and hiding Scripture in our hearts begins lifelong change as we meditate on God's Word and then wait with this passage. Maybe you will memorize it—write it on a three-by-five card and carry it with you, or tape it on a mirror or your dashboard or your kitchen window or put it in your back pocket. Maybe you will simply read it and wait with God's words, holding them like a chocolate drop beneath your tongue. Ask God to bring out the flavors of this passage, to highlight a word or phrase for your soul, and to help you apply this passage to your life. This is where transformation happens.

transparency through prayer

These words are a prayer, a heartfelt rending of the curtain that separates us from God and from our selves. These prayers offer some words to take you into deeper honesty with God. Healing happens when we identify with the encounter with Jesus and then pray through our own issues.

transpired action

Just for today, how will you live? What will change as a result of your encounter with Jesus? How will these illuminations shine into your soul and out of your life into this world? What action will take place?

If you, too, often feel like a dim wick or a wet log, welcome. You are in good company! But be prepared. These ten encounters with Jesus will take your breath away; they will be like billows to the smoldering coals—they will set you on fire with the Light of the World. And then you will shine.

come along
to the river

Illuminations on Relationship

"This is my Son, whom I love;
with him I am well pleased."
—MATTHEW 3:17

We must have some room to breathe....
Our relationships are being starved to
death by velocity. No one has the time to
listen, let alone love. Our children lay
wounded on the ground, run over by
our high-speed good intentions.
—RICHARD SWENSON

The gadget fits in my ear, the size of a cicada and about as annoying. Nearly as light as a fig leaf, it feels fragile and innocuous, but its purpose is to turn me into a work-all-the-time automaton. In the former days, it was enough to just get from point A to point B without solving the mysteries of the universe or at least the issues of waste management, without creating endless lists of to-dos for the return to home base.

Now, we drive from point A to point B, smooshing in C, D, and E for efficiency's sake, all the while making sure the batteries for the phone and earpiece are charged so we can continue working…um…I mean *communicating*. Because don't these gadgets help us keep in touch?

Yesterday I flapped around like a distracted Big Bird for five minutes trying to gather all the information for calls I needed to make on the twelve-minute drive to a lunch meeting (and all the errands on the way). Rather than simplifying my life, this communication device plays into my rule-bound being: I should make the most of every single minute, even if it raises my anxiety to espresso-level jitters.

Can't we just drive anymore?

No. Because we are driven women, with an unwritten rule book encompassing all thought and behavior. *Always, never, should,* and *ought* dictate our days and caffeinate our nights. Our eyeballs jump like kids on a hotel bed, should we dare lower our lids. The specter of our undones and poorly dones drives us; the voices of people in our past and our present remind us of the guidelines carved in stone. Like the old song, "Do this, don't do that, can't you read the sign?"

Oh, we can read the signs just fine. We just can't live by them anymore.

These rules in stone were never designed to bring us life. They were intended to remind us of how impossible it is to live this life, how far short we fall of the mark, how desperately we need relief from all the rules and regulations whispering their guilty messages into our souls.

Come along. Rush to the river, and meet the One who will change everything, absolutely everything, about our rule-bound living.

breaking news

After centuries of revelation from God and revolution from the Israelites, the last prophet closes his mouth. For four hundred years, God keeps quiet. No prophets prophesy, no miracles dazzle. No signs, no wonders. "The people walking in darkness," the prophet Isaiah wrote, predicting this bleak interlude (9:2). Long darkness—darkness since people started avoiding eye contact with God and either focusing on the rules or avoiding the rules altogether, creating total darkness. Then, hunched over in their shadows, perched on the haunches of wordlessness, they hear it.

In the middle of nowhere, an Old Testament look-alike prophet bellows out some new good news. After generations of silence, dead silence on God's part, at last a voice. From out of the desert comes this new word for people who have been waiting for generations.

"Repent, for the kingdom of heaven is near," calls out John (Matthew 3:2).

The people churn a wake of dust as they rush to the wilderness to see this wild man in camel-hair garb and leather belt. They have waited in the blackout silence for so long.

Squinting against the desert sun, seeking a brightness to illuminate their shadows, they rustle through the sand with expectancy, with heart-thrumming anticipation. Surely they wonder, "Is this the time, at long last? Is this the Messiah?"

From Jerusalem and Judea and the whole region of the Jordan River, the people hustle to hear the word and draw near to that kingdom. Their faces shine with the expectation of rescue. People crowd around, all ears, ready for newness, ready for change.

They press toward John, and God presses on their hearts, and they begin to open to the possibility of hope—not hope in John. Hope in the One to whom he points. "I baptize you with water for repentance. But after me will come one who is more powerful than I.... He will baptize you with the Holy Spirit and with fire" (Matthew 3:11).

Imagine their deep breaths, the reality settling like cold water into a sauna full of hot sand, seeping in through their pores and their ears and their minds, running through their circulatory systems. Finding lodging in their hearts, fresh hope for a new day, for relief from the woes of a people stooped over from a centuries-long dark night of the soul.

fulfilling all righteousness

From the waters of the Jordan, John sees him. The Hope. The Light. "After me will come one...," says John, "whose sandals I am not fit to carry" (verse 11).

Paintings over the centuries depict Jesus and John together, often with curly red hair, as babies, toddlers, children playing, laughing. As cousins, perhaps they did see each other, at least at the Feast of the Passover, surely at some of the annual ceremonies and celebrations in Israelite life and faith.

But now, the scene shifts. And Jesus is no longer John's cousin. Jesus is his Lord.

Jesus steps up to John and asks to be baptized. John, preaching about baptism and repentance, and here is the sinless One, asking to be baptized? He must be speechless, his heart must just stop for a split second, before protesting, "I need to be baptized by you, and do you come to me?" (verse 14). As though John is saying, "No way do I baptize you. I, in all my sinfulness, need to repent and be baptized by you. You are the holy One, the long-awaited Redeemer."

But here, by the Jordan, in the middle of the glaring desert sun, Jesus offers hope—bright, burnished hope: "Let it be so now; it is proper for us to do this to fulfill all righteousness" (verse 15).

Jesus is saying, *In my baptism, I step into the waters and identify with your sin and shame. I say yes to God's plan for me and our plan for you—that I, in my righteousness, take on your sin, and thus fulfill all righteousness. All the demands of the Law.*

To fulfill all righteousness. Jesus came to fulfill all the jots and tittles of the rules and the laws—to satisfy the bill, like a warehouse would do when an order is presented. "I need holiness. I need absolute satisfaction of all the demands of the 613 rules in the Torah."[1] And the Christ comes, full of grace, full of truth, and absolutely able to fulfill the Law and the Prophets (see Matthew 5:17).

To fulfill all righteousness! It seems almost too good to be true. I want to turn cartwheels; I want to leap about and get on my knees and sing and lead cheers and tell everyone, everywhere. Because this means we can take a deep breath. It means that we are perfect only through Jesus, not because we keep a perfectly straight house or always utter the perfect words to loved ones and strangers, not because we perfectly evangelize or perfectly raise our kids or perfectly do anything. We absolutely cannot perfectly do anything.

Except, even in our imperfections, we can come to Jesus—and that is perfect. There, when we look at him, we move into his perfection. We step into his righteousness and into the fulfillment of all he came to do.

Do you see it? Do you see the sparkle of hope illuminating the shadows? We are on the water's edge of the source of real radiance. In fact, the Scriptures tell us that real radiance is here, right now. "The Son is the radiance of God's glory and the exact representation of his being, sustaining all things by his powerful word" (Hebrews 1:3).

shower of delight

So John agrees to Jesus's request and baptizes the One whose sandals John is not good enough to carry. He grips Jesus's shoulders and lowers him into the waters of the Jordan River, the very river that separated the Israelites from the Promised Land, the same waters that separated to bring them into freedom.

Jesus parts the water with his body, and when he rises, the people glimpse heaven in the desert. The beginning of the fulfillment of all righteousness. As river water streams from Jesus, the heavens split apart. The Spirit of God, like a radiant floating dove,

flutters down and alights on this Man who already weaves longing around a mesmerized crowd.

And the voice of God showers down from heaven, "This is my
Son, whom I love; with him I am well pleased" (Matthew 3:17).
"This is My beloved Son, in whom I am well-pleased" (NASB).

The waters and the heavens split apart in delight for the coming of this One who would forever change the rules. This One
who would reinstitute the missing ingredient in the world of his
day, and the world of ours: relationship. With God.

God's words about Jesus are more than a benediction, a "saying well" of someone, for that is literally what *bene* ("well") and
diction ("speaking") mean. God's words are also an inauguration,
as when the most powerful person in a country announces the suc-
cessor, a public presentation of a new ruler. But it is more than that
as well, though God's words do serve as the initiation of Jesus's
public ministry.

Because God doesn't say, "I'm well pleased in what he will do,
what he came to earth to do." He doesn't say, "I *will* be well
pleased when Jesus does what he came to do." No. Not in the
works Jesus would do, for this is present tense. And not in Jesus's
purpose. God says, "In *him* I am well pleased. Delighted, just
thrilled."

God is delighted in the person of Jesus. Jesus hasn't done one
thing yet—and still God is well pleased.

the One we've been waiting for

This is hard for me to grasp, what with my long list of to-dos
gripped between my pincers, the steering wheel in one hand, a cup

of coffee in the other hand, the cicada-shaped phone chirping in my ear, and wrinkles between my eyebrows while I steer with my knee. Jesus hasn't done anything, and God is well pleased. What a contrast between my rushing about, embracing all the rules for Christian living, and Jesus's receiving God's blessing.

This is the Man I want to encounter, the One I've been waiting for, while I've focused on my tasks and ticked off my accomplishments and wailed over my failures. I want to meet up with this Jesus who fulfilled all righteousness on my behalf.

Because I, too, stand at the desert's edge, the air a hot furnace on my face, my own heart run ragged by my misguided expectations of myself and others. And at this desert's edge, on the bank of the River Jordan, I must examine what isn't working...because this way of living isn't working.

It's like playing some contorted version of Twister—right hand on the red circle, left foot on green, swing backward and put your left hand on yellow and move your right foot over your head to blue. We are emotional contortionists trying to fit into every person's requirements and a long list of our own rules to live by. After all, we should be all things to all people, right? Surely this is the Christian way to live.

Or is it?

We live this way poorly, awkwardly, with some embarrassing falls, ridiculous positions, and bruised relationships. Nothing glamorous or sexy about a twisted ankle or a frayed, tattered, fibrillating heart from trying to meet all the expectations we, our family, our church, our society heap upon us.

The result? High blood pressure or stress eating or colitis or migraines. This twisted living plays havoc with our families, our marriages, our service in the church and in the world. People may quit playing with us in our own version of Twister, because they can't figure out how to meet the often-unspoken demands of all our rules.

shouldering the shoulds

For the past year I've collected the shoulds that women share with me. The list weighs a thousand pounds in terms of its load on our shoulders. And yet rules are helpful. We need speed limits. We need to know that the mail carrier will not ever pick up the mail from the blue drop box before the posted time. We need a due date on that bill. Rules are meant to help us know how and when to act. They help us understand what is expected of us.

This is part of the problem. The alwayses and nevers, the shoulds and oughts help us feel safe. We know what to do because someone, somewhere, lined out the expectation, set the standard. Rules mean we can live a black-and-white life, always knowing which is the right side. And when we feel like we are meeting the requirements for life, filling in all the blanks correctly, there's a sense of acceptance and approval. We made the club. We're okay.

But this is a club that Jesus came to disband. The self-righteous "I did everything right" assembly of people who don't need help, don't need anything except their bootstrap belief. *They* surely don't need a Savior.

Though the Chinese custom of foot binding ended in the early twentieth century,[2] we practice our own type of binding with our hidden requirements for ourselves and others. These high standards and expectations may seem good, as innocuous as gossamer, but wrap them around yourself enough times and you're immobilized. The more layers, the more paralyzed. When female children in China were bound, sometimes the adults broke four toes on each foot before wrapping those little girls' soft, uncalloused feet. Otherwise, those toes broke within a year, leaving only the big toe intact. Ultimately, their four- to six-inch-long feet rendered the young women unable to work, unable to function, with difficulty even in walking.

Does not our soul binding do the same for us? With enough binding comes breaking of the spirit, and incapacity to function results. Like the Chinese custom, our soul binding may begin when we are young, fresh-faced children of five or six or seven. As in the painful foot binding practice, growth is not only hindered but ultimately halted.

The consequences add up. We continue to raise the bar on what is acceptable behavior, and guess what: no one ever meets our standards; no one can ever please us. Beneath all this lurks the sense that we cannot please anyone without total perfection. Certainly not God.

Our rushing bulldozes relationships. We rely on rules to keep us on the rails and in favor with God and others, rather than relying on God's love to create in us a love response of obedience. We've lost God's longing for us, as Isaiah shows.

God will speak to this people, to whom he said, "This
is the resting place, let the weary rest"; and, "This is the
place of repose"—but they would not listen. So then,
the word of the LORD to them will become: Do and do,
do and do, rule on rule, rule on rule; a little here, a little
there—so that they will go and fall backward, be injured
and snared and captured." (28:11–13)

I'm tired of all the do and do. Jesus is our resting place, and
only as we encounter him through our days will we find the rest
we seek. Never in the rules, the expectations, the rushing. Only
in meeting with Jesus. But how do we get there? Where do we
find him?

Come along. It isn't far.

the river's edge

Every day begins at the edge of the desert, right there with Jesus
alongside the bank of the River Jordan. Every day, we get to step
into Jesus's righteousness as we roll out of bed—dismantling our
need to be perfect, pretty, pleasing, or whatever else makes up the
never-ending chorus in our head.

After all, Jesus didn't rush out into the ministry God had for
him, like a runner from the starting block. He stepped into the
river of God's delight and anointing and then went to the desert
(see Matthew 4).

Can we go to the river with Jesus and meet up with him
there, with his delight and anointing, before rushing into the day?

What if every time we are near water, like in the shower, or washing our hands or the dishes, or drinking from a water fountain, or watering flowers, we say, as a former pastor said, "Remember our baptism"? That pastor sprinkled water over the people joining the church and invited them to step back into the river, to remember the moment when they were identified with Jesus. Because at our baptism, we enter into Christ's cleansing work, Christ's perfection (to fulfill all righteousness!), his total *enoughness*. Not our own *enoughness* at all.

a day starter

Of course, every single day, we start with a list: plot our to-dos, chart our chores, tally our tasks. Get to work, clean the house, prepare the meals, make all the lunches before your first cup of coffee, care for the children, poke them into their snowsuits and boots, and herd them out the door for school…

What if instead we begin with, not what we need to *do*, but who we want to *be* today?

Who do you want to be in your relationships? And how do you get there? Only by encountering Christ throughout the day can you find out.

Try this: Go ahead and make your list, jot down your jobs; then stop. Take five minutes and be totally still. Reflect on God's words to Jesus at his baptism: "This is my Son, whom I love; with him I am well pleased."

Can you hear God say this over you?

At a women's weekend, Constance tried this. She listed her

anxieties: surgery on Monday, a procedure she'd had five years ago with a one-in-a-million chance of repeating it. She'd battled decades of depression, illness, and pain. And now this...

At the end of our retreat, we paused for five minutes. Though worries and pain crowded her brain, into the litany sliced four words: *I'm proud of you.* All other thoughts fled.

I'm proud of you.

In all her years of loving God, of serving Christ, she'd never once heard Jesus say, "I'm proud of you." So she wept—cried at this intimate encounter with him, these sweet words of affirmation and encouragement at such a critical life juncture.

Go ahead and try this yourself. Take five. Today, and then tomorrow, and then the next day. Even if you don't hear a literal voice speaking, giving Jesus the gift of silence takes us out of the rushing realm and into the place where God is in control. See what happens, see if you begin to encounter Jesus increasingly throughout your day.

When a woman encounters Jesus, she is changed. By considering who we will be today (for instance, "Today I want to be more lovely to everyone I meet"), then we know what we need: we need to be loved. Because women who are loved become lovely, and more loving. So that brings us to the place where we must learn to be present with Jesus and in his love. Like Constance.

And then, when you realize you have failed to be more lovely, more loving, start over. Say you do all your dos and you're ugly in the process—where did you need to meet Jesus along the way?

What we do must proceed from who we are—and who we are is loved. We can start over every single second, if need be. Reroute your mind and heart. Go back to that River, listen to those words again: "I am well pleased." "I am proud of you."

Can you hear that? We need a rewrite on our rules, because this is definitely not how we live. Our thought processes work something like this:

We start out with a happy little tune.

Jesus loves me.
This I think I know...or I heard that somewhere
For the Bible tells me so. I should believe it, anyway...

But look at my house—it's a wreck. Why can't I keep it clean? And look at my office—talk about *behind.* If I were any further behind I'd be lapping myself. And why am I not married? Or why *am* I married? Or why is my marriage such a traffic wreck? If only I had children, or if only the kids were doing better in school, or were more respectful, or helpful around the house, or picked up their own mess... When was the last time I served a meal that didn't come from a carton?

No wonder we don't shine.

Before we go further, let's go back to the River. Listen to that voice again, and put your name in that place.

This is my daughter, whom I love. In her I am well pleased. Do you hear the pride? the delight? the absolute, turning-cartwheels love splitting open heaven and alighting on you? On *you.*

Now go look in the mirror. Yes, the splotchy bathroom mirror, or the fingerprinted one in the dining room. And say those words again, listen to them, one more time. Say them until they begin to be real, not just words:

This is my daughter, whom I love. In her, I am well pleased.

It's enough to make you glow.

come along to...

 • transfer from dark to light •

Oh, God,
I want to shift my eyes away from your gaze.
Your eyes are so bright and
So much darkness fills me.
There is no room for radiance.
And I am tired of all the rules I try to live by,
Worn out by my rushing.
Weary of the games I play, trying to be good enough.
Because I am not good enough.
And I confess that, knowing
That Jesus
Is good enough.
He is all I need.
Forgive me for trying to play it perfect
When Jesus just wants me to hear your voice,
Your delight, your love.

Thank you for being the one place
Where I am truly loved
Without performance.

• transfix upon Christ •

Relax into God's presence now. Breathe deeply, and rest there. Put away the rules that you should be always busy, always working, always earning your keep, and let God love you.

• translate the meaning •

- What shoulds do you carry around with you? Where did you learn these, and how are they reinforced, and by whom? What benefits do you receive from your rules?
- Consider your rushing: What is beneath it? When do you feel most rushed? What has the rush cost you?
- Think back on some of the silent times, when God did not speak and darkness surrounded you. Maybe this is a dark time too. What brought on the darkness?
- When do you feel most alive, most hopeful?
- Whose voice do you hear affirming you, loving you? Or does the voice you listen to suggest that you are not worth loving, that no good dwells in you, that you are a failure? How can you respond to both voices?

• transform by renewing your mind •

May God himself, the God of peace, sanctify you through and through. May your whole spirit, soul and body be kept blameless at the coming of our Lord Jesus Christ. The one who calls you is faithful and he will do it.

1 Thessalonians 5:23–24

• transparency through prayer •

Dear Lord,
The list is long and dull,
And I am tired.
Tired of my perfectionism,
Tired of others' perfectionism
And rushing, tired of the shoulds,
Tired of the alwayses and nevers and oughts
That go along with them.
So I choose, now,
Today,
To let go of my list-driven life
And instead
Turn to Jesus
Who came "to fulfill all righteousness."
Light me with your love
That I might be radiant,
Just like you.

In Jesus's good name,
Amen.

• transpired action •

How will you notice and let go of your rushing today?

come along
to the temple

Illuminations on Transparency

"Has no one condemned you?…
Then neither do I condemn you,"
Jesus declared. "Go now
and leave your life of sin."
—JOHN 8:10–11

Nothing makes us so lonely
as our secrets.
—PAUL TOURNIER

They are alone. They are in a group. They are pensive, dreamy, restive, festive, laughing, lounging. They are picnicking, boating, rowing, reading. They are in places where mothers would say, "Don't get your dress dirty!" and they wear the unthinkable: white.

In impressionist art, these women appear in their airy, petti-coated, ruffled, and bowed white dresses. They have no fear of grass stains or sand or dirt. In their unblemished white, dappled only with the shadows of the trees, they stand in stark relief from the dark-garbed men, the heavy colors of nature. They are women, forever in white, forever unstained, forever enjoying life as ladies of leisure.

White in apparel has been a standard no-no ever since I started washing my own laundry, because I have no faculty for stain removal, whether green from grass, or red from blood, or brown from coffee or chocolate or probably both. And after our children's births, the stain trouble doubled, tripled, and quadru-pled between burps and spit ups and drools and food drop-pings—to say nothing of all the other don't-mention-at-meals substances that permanently stain babies' clothing.

Further, if you turned on the tap in our first home, orange liquid dribbled and then spurted from the spout. The tub, the toi-let, the sinks all took on the hue of Halloween regardless of the season. White clothing and rusty water do not a happy marriage make.

Though I grew up with the social standard of wearing white only between Memorial Day and Labor Day, as an adult my apparel rule became "Thou shalt not wear white. Ever." I didn't want people to see that I'm messy, inept. This goes for my soul as well. White—emotional white, spiritual white—allows people to see, know, judge; and then the jig is up; all sins, flaws, the evi-dence of a stained soul are on public display.

Come along to an early-morning meeting, to peek in on

another public but intimate, illuminating encounter with Jesus, and a woman whose faults ended up on public display.

muddied and stained

Where were they, these spying men who pried her from her lover's arms and hauled her at dawn to the temple? Were they hiding in the bushes? And who turned her in, anyway? Did they set her up, arrange for the man to seduce her?

Questions must whirl at her mind and eat away at her insides as the men yank her through the streets in her just-from-bed attire, or lack of attire, and propel her in front of the Teacher. She wants to cover herself, to hide her body from view, to cloak her shame, but can only stand, stripped of her pride, her good name, her hope and future. Emotionally naked, totally vulnerable, she flinches at the words from the mob of red-faced men.

The Pharisees and scribes demand of Jesus, "Teacher, this woman was caught in the act of adultery. In the Law Moses commanded us to stone such women. Now what do you say?" (see John 8).

She cannot cover up, cannot camouflage the truth: they caught her in adultery. She awaits the death penalty, stoning.

What about her husband? What about her children? What does death by stoning feel like? Is it gradual, or instant? Does she suffocate, or die from head trauma? If she loses consciousness, will she still feel the pain of the blows? Will her family ever recover from the shame of her actions?

She sucks in her breath, waiting for his answer, unable to drag her gaze away from this man with the deep, caring eyes.

She has heard of him, the miracles, the mumblings of the men around town. She bows her head, bracing for the inevitable. Her body trembles, shock shaking through her veins, turning her to ice. Knowing she deserves death intensifies her fear.

As though Jesus hasn't heard them, as though oblivious to the scene before him, he answers the men's questions with silence. Then he bends down, writing in the dirt with his finger.

The men hurl more questions at him, a verbal pouncing.

The woman listens carefully, feeling like a pawn in a game whose stakes she cannot totally comprehend. Her life is at stake, but this feels bigger than that.

Jesus ignores the questions, writing in the sand. Finally, he stands. He meets the angry stare of each accuser, looking carefully around the circle. His words fall with a thud: "If any one of you is without sin, let him be the first to throw a stone at her." Then again he stoops, writing on the ground.

The questions splutter away into silence—shocked, shamed silence. The oldest of the men lowers his head. His shoulders sag. He turns, slowly, as though his anger has sunk into his feet and turned them to stone. The others drop their chins, one by one. Staring at the ground, they turn and leave, one by one.

And she is left, standing, alone. Alive.

The Teacher looks up from where he perches on his heels. Looks around, as though surprised. "Woman, where are they? Has no one condemned you?"

She struggles to find her voice, chokes out the words, "No one, sir."

"Then neither do I condemn you," Jesus declares.

free

No condemnation? Wonder, disbelief, fear, joy intermingle, an intoxicating blend of emotions that set her feet to dancing and her heart to singing. She has been set free!

So it is for us, as well. Jesus's words, "Neither do I condemn you," catapult us into the midst of a full-blown orchestral arrangement of Romans 8:1: "There is therefore now no condemnation to those who are in Christ Jesus" (NKJV).

No condemnation? Breathe in that fresh air. Drag all of your sins through your scarred soul and out through your mind and your mouth as you write them down or speak them aloud. Go ahead. List the shames that haunt you, the pain that taunts you, the ugly leering voice that declares you to be worthless, "dead in your trespasses and sins" (Ephesians 2:1, NASB). Haul those out, into the daytime, and let the brilliance of Christ's declaration spill over you, a golden glow of light and lightness. Trumpet along with Charles Wesley's famous hymn, "And Can It Be?":

> No condemnation now I dread;
> Jesus, and all in him, is mine;
> Alive in him, my living Head,
> And clothed in righteousness divine,...
> 'Tis mercy all, immense and free,
> For O my God, it found out me!

Make your list. Jesus closed the encounter with this woman with, "Go now and leave your life of sin." You can leave the life of sin when you hear him, deep at the bottom of your soul, say, "Neither do I condemn you."

Yet hearing those words is one thing. It's another to ask…

go where?

Where does this woman go after hearing Jesus? Her sin becomes a public spectacle, and then, in the middle of the religious center, she is forgiven. Not condemned! How can that be? Clearly by Law she is guilty and deserving of death. And yet this man looks through her guilty eyes and into her soul, and offers her freedom, offers her another chance, offers to clear her record and grant her life.

The same scenario plays out for each of us today. The key to living in freedom from guilt and shame—to recovery from uncovering the sickness of our sin—is transparency. Vulnerability. Yes, wearing white. When Jesus forgives, this woman no longer needs to cover up, camouflage, the current or past state of her soul.

Part of shame is the secrecy of our sin when we hide it versus "confess your sins to each other and pray for each other so that you may be healed" (James 5:16). Secrecy and freedom are often mutually exclusive. But when we truly experience Jesus's words— "Neither do I condemn you"—the release from condemnation leads us to transparency. If Jesus doesn't condemn us, then we must learn to not condemn ourselves and not allow others to condemn us, either. Nor can we afford, then, to condemn others.

Knowing Jesus's delight in us (so clearly unmerited), we can be vulnerable about our weaknesses, transparent because we are so loved, so forgiven. Our transparency grants others freedom to open their wounded hearts and begin to hope again, begin to breathe, begin to heal.

go now...leave your life of sin

For this woman, freed from death, leaving her life of sin will include not only no more adultery but also no vengeance toward the men who showcased (and possibly even set up) her sin in order to best another man.

So for her, she needs to get rid of her shame. For me, shame means entering default mode and leads to a rupturing of my relationship with God, self, and others—and this is sin, though we inevitably go there, like a self-propelled train on preset rails. For the woman Jesus addressed, this meant letting go of her outright sin of sleeping with a man who was not her husband—and letting go of her inevitable fury over being so callously put on display, her inner workings turned into a public vehicle.

Perhaps we would all live more transparent lives if we thought of sin as a public display, but also always saw ourselves in light of Jesus's forgiveness. No one in that circle of shame and venom deserved forgiveness, but they all got a second chance...or ninetieth or one thousand and ninety third.

The choice is, always, to "go now and leave your life of sin."

sharing our secrets

Instead, too much of the time, we have generations of women walking around with lips curved upward in a smile that covers teeth gritted from pain or anger; women, from young to old, trying to love the people in their lives and serve them; women trying to be the perfect Christian "little woman," trying not to get it wrong, not hurt anyone or offend or make waves.

What are the secrets these women hide? Abortions, broken or disappointing marriages, stepfamilies, prodigal children, abuse—whether physical, sexual, or emotional.

And there are also the women who have given up trying. These are the women who have thrown down their cards, surrendered all hope of ever making a dent in real life, ever being truly loved, ever being free to be the women God created. Their frustration levels hit pressure-cooker highs, and rather than blow, they leave—the church, or marriage, or job, or faith, or even their children. Or they live simply as custodians, the body's shell marking their place in the universe and in the family system, like a pawn on the chessboard, but their hearts have evaporated. No one is home anymore. Church didn't work for them, not the patterned-and-printed-fabric churches of today where everyone needs to be fine for the gospel to be true.

Women who don't care also slip into the pews or evacuate them. They haven't figured out how to make room for others in their lives, how to break out of the shell of their own satiation and needs. They may be glowing from a tanning bed but not from their encounters with Jesus.

We have women who more than anything in the world need a safe place, a spot where they can let down their pretenses, a place where they can voice their disappointments, discouragement, despondency; a place where it's okay to not be okay, and to admit it.

Yes, women have wounds, and we act out of our woundedness and our sin in anger, adultery, passivity, coldness.

What if, instead, we cut the camouflage, quit disguising our wounds, and made them open? What if we began to heal, and gave others permission to begin to heal as well, bringing us out of the darkness, shame, and pain of the past and even present?

cut the camouflage

The woman caught in adultery was, in a sense, forced to do this—to "wear white" and publicly disclose her sin. The result: instant transparency and vulnerability. Unlike white garments, patterned clothing creates a camouflage for our reality, the opposite of transparency. If we're bleeding, no one notices right away. If the seat wears thin, or a tiny piece of seam opens, or we dribble our juice, it isn't as obvious. This is true of our souls as well: patterns and prints, emotionally speaking, cover our rips, spills, and spots. If we're torn or stained, others can't see as easily the truth, the klutziness or messiness, of our lives—the fall there, the cut here, the infection there. The wounds that we carry about hide in the folds and flowers of our emotional clothing—in our niceness, politeness, and that's-all-right-ness—so others never really know the impact of their words or actions on us.[1]

But if we're wearing white and begin to bleed, they notice. The grass stains show, the muddy knees, the pilling and the pulling. "Ouch, that hurts," says our white clothing with the stains seeping through. Our pain is evident, our wounds apparent.

When we don't wear white emotionally, our outsides, our florals and finesse, cover death; our tight-lipped smiles stretch over hearts that are tombs. Though this goes against our rules, we need a place where we can wear white year round.

The more I know Jesus, the more I hear his words, the more I think, *Jesus wore white.* He was a plain talker, famous for not playing the political correctness game; totally secure in being God's Beloved. That resulted in a transparency, a speaking of the truth that is far from our churchy reality (or unreality) today. Jesus wore white: the pure white of absolute authority, and sinlessness, and clarity of purpose. He wore the white of single-minded love and life. He wore the white clothes of heaven.

the spectacle

Don't let this talk of whiteness lead to some kind of public spectacle with another at the center. So often we are interested in uncovering (taking the covers off!) another's sin, *not* for the purpose of repentance and restoration and godly living, but for the purpose of discrediting, judging, lifting ourselves up by unveiling another's defects. Those men in the temple are not interested in the woman's redemption. They don't care about whether she lives a holy life, whether she knows God's delight and joy in her. They are interested in discrediting Jesus and don't mind stripping her in the middle of the temple to further their own evil ends.

There is a lesson here. Airing another's sin could easily be about our power and even self-righteousness rather than repairing the wounds of living in a fallen world, in less-than-perfect relationships. These scribes and Pharisees, threatened by Jesus and wanting to find a means to legally persecute him, cannot afford to have their own hearts exposed, so they drop their stones and drop their charges and walk away, reminded of their sinful state.

In reality, perhaps the accusers show rare and remarkable

integrity when they leave the stoning circle. They have done battle with their souls and the presence of God and lost. Or, perhaps,
they have won, because God won. They could not, in all honesty,
condemn this woman because they were not without sin.

What relief in knowing that we are not alone in our sinful
state, in our shame, in our mistakes and missteps. What relief,
then, it brings to wear white, to live in the truth of "no condemnation."

when women wear white

On an emotional plane, white allows for transparency. Honesty.
White signifies a willingness to take a risk; it suggests direct communication rather than innuendos and hidden agendas—very
much like Jesus, really.

Wearing white is refreshing and contagious. Imagine if we all
began to be more honest in our relationships, more open about
our wounds, hurts, and hopes. Imagine what this would do for
the body of Christ. Women who must get their own way and
don't mind hurting others to do so would at last hear how their
behavior hindered Christ's transformation in others. They would
be invited, at last, into a kindness and grace that are not about
power or control.

Wearing white would mean a lack of artifice and the presence
of honesty. People wouldn't leave the church due to hurt feelings
or because they didn't fit in with all the other "perfect" people
there, because wearing white would mean hurt feelings would be
known and discussed and people open and forgiving about imperfections. Loneliness would abate as we all found friends who

understood, since they know well their own "less-thans." Marriages would be transformed, people would stop playing mind-reading games—the old "if you don't know, I'm certainly not going to tell you."

Imagine how Jesus would feel about it. Maybe he'd heave a huge sigh of relief, a sigh big enough to carve out the Grand Canyon, enough to power white sails on a thousand ships, and say, "Finally, you get it."

So how does this work?

Practice with me: "Ouch, I felt hurt when you said that." "Whoa, my anger surprised me after your words, and here's what I discovered about myself…" "Want to go for a walk? I miss you." "I feel attractive and alive when you touch me." "I want to love you more but I am afraid sometimes." "Guilt torments me over my mistakes and prevents me from intimacy with you." "Today I felt sad after…" Fill in your own blank.

Will this be disconcerting to a husband or boyfriend, a friend or colleague? Your parents, siblings? Yes. Because when we wear white, when we practice identifying, owning, and being honest about the state of our own souls and hearts, an emotional transfer and maturing occur within us. We transfer emotional responsibility for our lives back where it belongs: on ourselves. We don't blame others for our feelings or wounds, but we do attach a "damaged inventory" sticker to their behavior, letting them know in the kindest way possible their impact on us.

Yesterday, when working alongside a friend, I felt hurt by her tone of voice and the look in her eye. I continued to work but withdrew emotionally, answering questions with the fewest possible words. Then I realized that to not tell her how I received her words meant I was choosing to avoid relationship. So I simply said, "I'm not sure you realize how judgmental you sounded just then. I agree with what you said, but the way you said it felt hurtful to me."

Horrified, she apologized immediately. She hadn't meant to sound critical at all, and hadn't intended anything negative. Wearing white keeps the cloth of relationships intact.

Wearing white also means that we don't saddle someone else with the burden and duty of making us feel good, or pretty, or worthy. That's too much weight to place on another, because ultimately, we are God's beloved and our very meaning, our value, comes from him. While his love for us often shows up through others, they are not responsible for how we feel. (They are, however, responsible for communicating in healthy or unhealthy ways, and this is again another entrance point for wearing white. Even just a simple response, such as, "If you could say it like this…, I could hear you better," keeps the dialogue loop open and eliminates blame.)

appropriate white

After all, is anything more tedious than people who constantly buttonhole us and press into us their feelings, needs, emotional woundedness, and our impact on them? Don't make this a thoughtless continual airing of your own low-self-esteem issues, like a fan that won't stop blowing. People will check their caller

ID and not answer your phone calls. They'll put you on their blacklist for e-mail. No one wants to be around people who are so supersensitive that every word becomes a matter of discussion, every inflection a means of hurt feelings.

We don't have to camp out on our white soapbox, making sure everyone in the universe knows how we feel and when we're hurt, choosing to interpret interactions in the worst possible light and not let go of an incident, not believing the best of the other person. In these instances, we need to ask, "Why do I interpret others' words in this way? Why can't I just move on?"

We must assess genuine damages that relationships incur. Patterns in relationship need to be addressed, but growing up includes knowing when and how much (and how often) to speak.

Everyone doesn't need to know the state of your soul. No need to put a blurb in the church bulletin or take out an ad in the local paper. But please don't misunderstand—there are places where we need to tell our stories so that others can begin to get free as well.

White is about transparency and an internal, personal knowing. Part of my journaling is a wearing of white: all those scribbles are often just my own soul babblings, trying to get to the bottom of my reactions and messiness, my self-sorrow and sin. Wearing white, directed personally, means that I do the soul work necessary to become whole, even if I don't ever address another person about our exchanges and problems. It's a little like wearing lovely, white, soft, silky undergarments. They are not for others' benefit. They are for my own femininity, my own heart. Just so, wearing white through personal reflection, through asking myself and God about my reactions and needs and pain, takes me more deeply to a place of peace, of radiance.

the costs and impact of wearing white

One of my friends has worn white for as long as I've known her. She quit playing games when she began to get well, when she quit drinking and started becoming honest. She speaks the truth without fear, always with a smile behind her voice, twinkling in her eyes. Not everyone can handle her wearing of white. Emotional white is alarming in a society that values appearance over soul.

But, as she learned, the costs of wearing anything other than white add up monumentally. Dishonesty destroys relationships, sucks away trust, until all that's left is a rushing wind tunnel that will blow the hat off your head. Without white, we are forever playing games, caught up in social rules and people pleasing. As individuals we're lost in the shadows, dappled by the darkness that comes from never truly knowing oneself, never reaching the place of honesty.

So white will cost us. Others may not want to see you wear white, because it reminds them of how dingy their own souls can be; the contrast underscores their blemishes. White makes others uncomfortable because when comparing whites, they might not match. If your white is brighter, theirs looks stained, as if it's been washed in tea.

And so our white highlights others' sin, and our own as well. Like my friend Lin, who brought her white dress for a banquet and then realized she had packed only a black slip. Black slip, white dress? No way. So it is with our souls: the black slip, sin, shows through our white garment, and if white looks like confession, or repentance, then that, too, sits poorly with some people. Vulnerability and disclosure go against some of the rules of the "Let's pretend" game, the camouflaging of soul needs and wounds.

Ah, but the impact of white! When I wear white outside on a hot day, I am instantly cooler than if I wear a dark color. Just so, white may start a refreshing move toward honesty and vulnerability with others. Consider the freedom others would feel if we begin to wear an emotional and spiritual white. Wearing white is an act of generosity, inviting others into a new, bright, clean, hopeful place. White is a gift of love. Wearing white is a step toward radiance.

If we wore white, I like to think that our electric bills would diminish because so much brightness would shine from our faces.

come along to...

 • transfer from dark to light •

Oh, Lord,
I stand in that circle of angry, red-faced people,
And I know I am guilty, I am not without sin.
You are absolutely pure and holy,
Nothing unclean spots your garments.
But my wounds bleed in public.
I am blemished, and I confess these stains
To you now.
The anger, the unforgiveness, the blame.

The hurt, the resentment, the shame.
And I release them to you.
You caught me red-handed
But do not condemn me.
You comfort me and then
Call me forward.
"Go, now...leave your life of sin..."
And I want to go, I want to leave that life,
I want to live purely, wholly, holy
No more excuses,
No more blame.
Clothe me in the white of transparency
And forgiveness
That I might be whiter than snow.

• transfix upon Christ •

All the reasons why you can't wear white, at least right now, rise up and flap against the lid of your heart. Don't try to close the lid. Just sit and let those reasons rise. And then be still. Rest in this safe place, this place of honesty and solace. Let Jesus be your comfort, your rest.

• translate the meaning •

- What clothing beliefs did you grow up with? How did you interpret them personally? ("I must dress right or Mother won't approve," or, "People like me if I look nice," or…)

- Who has condemned you? Who are your accusers? Do
  you hear the voice of someone long ago, or long dead, or
  in the present? When do you condemn yourself? How
  can you move away from both shame and blame, and
  "throw no stones" yourself?
- What people do you know who "wear white"? How do
  you respond to their transparency? When do you feel
  uncomfortable with their vulnerability, and is that
  because of the state of your own soul, or because of what
  is shared by the others? Why?
- What immediately comes to mind when you think about
  putting into practice this wearing of white? What would
  you need to talk about; where would you need to explain
  stains and rips? What are you trying to camouflage, emotionally and spiritually, when you don't wear white? Why?
- How will you respond if your wearing white isn't well
  received? How can you find encouragement and comfort
  in Christ?

• transform by renewing your mind •

But now you must rid yourselves of all such things as these: anger,
rage, malice, slander, and filthy language from your lips. Do not
lie to each other, since you have taken off your old self with its
practices and have put on the new self, which is being renewed in
knowledge in the image of its Creator.

Colossians 3:8–10

• transparency through prayer •

Dear Lord,
Please
Take my camouflage
And prints and patterns
That I wear to cover up my heart
And soul
And clothe me,
Too,
In the brightness of transparency,
Of honest responses in
Relationships
And the gentle grace
That comes with
Being clothed in and by Christ.
In his name,
Amen.

• transpired action •

How will you wear white today?

come along to the parade

Illuminations on Needs

"What do you want me to do for you?"
Jesus asked.
—MARK 10:51

Grant, Lord, that I may know myself
that I may know thee.
—AUGUSTINE

I was expert at gauging the temperature in a room: the emotions, the undercurrents of distress, or anger, or fear. I could second-guess every occupant's mood, and felt fairly adept at reading their minds.

This is great if one wants a gig at the county fair freak show or the lead role in a play about codependents. Unfortunately, I didn't have the faintest idea what *I* was thinking or feeling. I hadn't learned the fine art of personal reflection or even personal opinions in my formative years. Instead, I practiced reading others, which left me in an emotionally delayed, somewhat malformed or at least unformed place.

I could fake my way through most relationships, continuing to focus on others, which looks like a godly approach. But when I got married, suddenly I found myself in a duet, where mind reading was about as helpful as running a live wire through water. All my long-neglected character flaws rose to the surface. Anger and resentment and laziness that I hadn't known populated the cupboard of my soul. I was unable to be wrong, absolutely unwilling to take the blame for anything.

After two babies and a parsonage, I knew I needed help.

I also knew that it wasn't okay to have needs, not in the Jane Rubietta School of Fineness. Everyone else, after all, was fine. They didn't have needs. And if I, the pastor's wife, wasn't fine, then the world might fall apart. But I'm the one who nearly fell apart, because I denied my own humanness, my own brokenness. Unlike all the king's horses and all the king's men, though, Jesus can put us back together again.

Come along, then, and meet a man who dared break the "don't have needs" approach and found a Savior.

mercy

The man sits, alert, his senses finely tuned to the noise and movement on this busy Jericho street. Because he is blind, his life depends on the ability to know passersby are, well, passing by, so that he can beg. A crowd approaches—he can feel the earth shudder beneath him—and he listens intently. Through the hubbub, he discerns a voice cutting through all the rest, a voice of authority, of reason, of compassion. He has heard of this man, this Jesus. Instantly, the blind man joins the ruckus of words.

"Jesus, Son of David, have mercy on me!" he shouts. This is not a whispered prayer, not words uttered in the silent tomb of his own heart. No, he shouts.

This does not go over well with the general populace. "Shush! Be quiet!" They are stern in their rebuke, angry that a blind beggar would dare intrude into the crowd around Jesus and ask for, of all things, mercy. Like *that's* going to happen.

But Bartimaeus does not shush, will not keep quiet. He hollers out again, "Son of David, have mercy on me!" The footsteps stop, and then, the gift of words, the incredible invitation, slices through the shushing crowd: "Call him."

He throws away his cloak. If you were blind, you would never do this, because if you let go of your cloak, you lose your primary possession, the one thing that keeps you warm on a cold night, cushions your seat, pillows your head, perhaps even collects the fruit of your beggings.

No hesitation: he scrambles to his feet with the nimbleness born of desperation and hope. He is not begging for crumbs or coins. He is asking for what only one person can give him. The man who just walked down the road.

Bartimaeus moves carefully to where Jesus's voice sounded and halts in front of him.

"What do you want me to do for you?" Jesus asks.

What a world-opening, eye-opening question.

Bartimaeus sucks in a huge breath. This is it. It's all or nothing. And he leaps into that chasm called faith: "Rabbi, I want to see" (see Mark 10:46–51).

There it is, out in the open, for everyone else to see too. What gall! What temerity! What gumption for this beggar, this street person, to call out to the very Messiah, the miracle worker who walked the streets and talked with anyone, so different from a regular king or other royalty. To ask for a miracle, to ask to see.

one who serves

Jesus and his crowd are en route to Jerusalem, heading toward Passover, the time when ultimately, after people have thrown palm leaves on the ground and hosanna-ed Jesus, they will crucify him. Christ has just wrapped up a discussion with his disciples, who want to be assured of great seats in the kingdom of heaven. How must this feel to Jesus, heading toward death by crucifixion, to see the hearts of his disciples who wrangle and angle for the best seats in the house?

Jesus's answer to their finagling is, "Whoever wants to become great among you must be your servant, and whoever wants to be first must be slave of all. For even the Son of Man did not come to be served, but to serve, and to give his life as a ransom for many" (Mark 10:43–45).

Then on the way to the City of David, Jesus and his entourage enter Jericho. They are about ten or fifteen miles from their destination, perhaps a day's walk in hilly terrain. I can't imagine how Jesus feels. All that haranguing with the disciples, all those people constantly dogging his steps, all the word wars with the

Pharisees—these must be exhausting. Not only that, but Jesus knows this is not a country amble; he knows exactly what will happen at the end of the upward hike. When Christ hears the voice cut through the rabbling crowd, everything must disappear: the fatigue, the long walk, the grasping disciples, the inevitable thoughts of Jerusalem. And Jesus stops.

An important man, on an important mission, and he stops. The crowd surges into him, like a parade that forgot to watch the baton up ahead, but he stands firm.

In lives that outrun the pace car, in lives that always feel like a frantic race toward an unknown finish, this stopping speaks loudly.

Once again, Jesus shows by his very life what it means to serve, to love, to be the greatest and thus the least. He lives out his sermon to the disciples. He lives out his words about accepting the unacceptable (see Mark 10:13–16). He lives out love. He stops and pays attention to someone who has been ignored for years. In the midst of a stressful, taxing journey; in the middle of a crowd of people pleasers; smack-dab in the middle of the street, Jesus stops. He stops the procession to give the gift of attention, time, kindness, and, yes, of mercy.

If Jesus didn't stop, the blind man surely could not have chased him through the crowds, caught up with him, begged him for attention. When Jesus stopped, he honored a man whom the world wanted to silence, a man the world barely even noticed anymore.

the shushing crowd

The crowd noticed, but only when the beggar insisted on hollering. Their reaction to the man feels a little too…churchy…to me, as though we are uncomfortable with people who have needs. They are messy, loud, maybe smelly, need a bath or at least a tissue or a wet-wipe or a baby-sitter or a job. They have questions we can't answer, and frankly, we're more than uncomfortable. We're at a loss for words because we don't know why Jesus hasn't straightened out their trouble yet. It makes us wonder a little about who Jesus really is and if he is all he's cracked up to be and if he really cares. So we prefer that people not make a stink, thank you.

The crowd closes ranks. They rebuke Bartimaeus for calling out to Jesus, for causing a scene, for bothering them with his silly needs. It's much easier if the needy people are invisible and silent, along with their blindness. *Rebuke* is a strong word, the same word used of the disciples when the moms wanted to squeeze through the big-boy football huddle to get to Jesus and have their babies blessed by him. They rebuke the blind man. They ask him to shut up, no doubt with the kindest of intentions.

Bartimaeus, of course, insists. In fact, he shouts all the more: "Son of David, have mercy on me!"

Jesus astounds the crowd, with his words, "Call him." I imagine them being taken aback, sort of swaying backward like curtains in the wind and then rising to the occasion, forever playing the role of know-it-all.

"Cheer up!" What a tacky and lousy and lame thing for the crowd to say. Like they're patting the poor kid at the playground with the hand-me-down clothes and open wounds and bruises. "Cheer up, buster. The sun will come up tomorrow, and you'll still be blind and sitting on the side of the street, begging. But, yeah, cheer up, okay? Put on a happy face, if you don't mind. It's much less disturbing to our worldview. Besides, here's a crumb for you: the Parade Marshal is calling you."

There will always be flimflam people with lame responses, who just don't have the wisdom or depth, experience or compassion to come up with true comfort. The glib, patronizing words are part of living in a shallow, or at least unhealed, world, and there is just nothing we can do about it. To address it would mean that we look lame as well, and needy in the worst sense, needing to defend ourselves with chins jutted out, chips lodged in place on our shoulders.

But I love the way Bartimaeus handles it all. He cuts through the clatter of false cheer and throws aside his cloak and jumps to his feet.

Throws. Jumps. What a childlike response to Jesus's call.

And isn't that all he said we needed?

"Anyone who will not receive the kingdom of God like a little child will never enter it" (Mark 10:15).

expecting *perfect*

God's people, of course, have a tradition of perfect offerings: perfect lamb, or ram, or bird—no rheumy eyes, no limping, no cripples allowed. We bring this to our faith and think that we can only offer Jesus perfection.

That's the one thing that we cannot offer Jesus, or anyone else for that matter—perfection, because we are not perfect, or we would not need the Savior.

Church, Christianity, is not about fineness. It's for people who need help, people who have fallen and can't hit the target, let alone the bull's-eye. In other words, it's for everyone: you, me, your cousin, your mean old neighbor. The "I'm fine" line is finished in Christianity, as is playing the people-pleasing game, wanting people to intuit what we need when we may not even know ourselves. We are unable to admit we aren't fine, because of shame ("I must be a failure if I have needs or hopes or longings or dreams") or bad role-modeling or not understanding the bottom line. Everybody blows it; everybody falls short.

Why don't we communicate our needs, hurts, fears?

Good question. Whatever our answers, we end up one sick bunch of people: angry, oppressed, steaming, sick with intestinal issues or tummy problems or headaches, neck aches or tiny control issues like needing absolute command over every committee at church. We end up like the plastic Fisher-Price people from my childhood: Mr. and Mrs. Perfect, with their perfectly coifed hair and trim little bodies and their even trimmer children with perfect little plastic hair, and even a perfect little dog and perfectly clean sofa. But inside, they are perfectly hollow. Empty.

What do you need?

Thankfully, the good news is, you *don't* need to be fine.

abandoned no longer

The parade grinds to a halt when Jesus heeds the blind man's cry. With just this one stop in a long chain of events that comprise Jesus's life, mercy visits, mercy stays.

The man sitting alongside the road, who leaps to his feet in response to Jesus's call, was born into such hope. He is the son of Timaeus, which means "precious, valuable."[1] And Bartimaeus surely was, at one time, truly the son of Mr. Precious, and thus valuable himself. But where is his daddy now? Why is Bartimaeus squatting in the street, begging? What happened to the father, Mr. Precious, Mr. Valuable, that he has abandoned his son there on the roadside? What is this man's story? Does "son of Precious" have any abandonment feelings of his own?

We don't know if his parents are living or dead, if they too are poor and thus unable to support their son. We don't know if they threw him out in the street to make his own blind way, or if he begs to help support them in their old age. We do know that he is sitting in the sightless, endless dark, without protection, without any kind of life insurance, without a safety net, and apparently without parents nearby. We know that society essentially abandons the beggar, the street person, the transient; that hasn't changed over the years.

You may not be homeless, without parents, but, like Bartimaeus, every one of us is an abandonment veteran, in some big ways, in some small ways. People who were our friends left us high and dry, didn't vouch for us in a pinch, didn't stand by our side during a time of flooding waters. People who assassinated your character, believed the worst about you when only the best was intended. Parents who were imperfect—in other words, all parents—inevitably leave some abandonment scars on their children. A spouse who was supposed to hang with you through better or worse left when things slid south.

As my friend says, "We all need to experience abandonment sometime in our life so we will turn to God, who will never abandon us."

And that is where the mercy enters. That is where the compassionate assistance of the Son of David seeps in. When we press through our abandonment, scramble toward hope, leap toward sight.

"Jesus, Son of David, have mercy on me!"

Though he could not see, he knew. Though blind, Bartimaeus saw who Jesus really was. Tough, poor castoff, sitting on the lowest rung of society, this man understood more than the seeing crowd of politician-loving, popularity-seeking gimmes. He an-nounced what others could not, had not. With eyes of faith, he called out the truth: this is the one who saves, this is the Son of David, this is the One.

And that One stops, waits, and asks, "What do you want me to do for you?"

you want what?

Hear that question again, that wondrous question from Jesus: "What do you want me to do for you?" He does not ask, like a weary parent, "What do you want *now*? Don't I feed you, provide clothes for you, shuttle you to ballet and ball practice, tuck you in bed, bring you water? What *now*?"

He asks, with the patience of all eternity, while time swirls to a stop around him, "What do you want me to do for you?"

Bartimaeus's plea is personally directed. He doesn't demur, doesn't shuffle around raising dust, doesn't scuff his feet and say,

"Well, never mind, it's really presumptuous and preposterous of me to ask this. I don't really need anything after all." He doesn't succumb to the "shut-upping" of the crowd. He doesn't ask a "bless the world" prayer. He just puts his whole trembling heart and life in the open: "Have mercy on *me*. Rabbi, I want to see."

I am convinced that seeking personal healing begins a ripple effect that could run around the world almost as fast as spam e-mails. But people will be uncomfortable with our needs, uneasy with our pain, blindness, and problems. They will, in various ways, ask us to "shut up." But Bartimaeus dares to ask for his needs to be met and does not let the shushers worry him. He does what he knows he can do: beg—for mercy, for sight.

When all the fat and falderal drain away, this is all we can do too: beg. We have no reason to expect anything. Yet we too have this man, this Messiah, who will stop, who says to us, "What do you want me to do for you?"

What, then, do you need? Can you put your face to the floor and wait until you can formulate a very direct answer to that question? Can you sit with it, awkward as it is, as needy and sick as you feel, and wait? What do you need? The answer is *not*, "Nothing." The answer cannot possibly be, "I'm fine." Because, remember? Jesus didn't come to call the healthy; he came for the sick. That certainly describes me. And maybe you too.

And can you allow Jesus to answer, in his time, in his way? The answer may not be the one you sought. He may not seem to grant your request. But our God knows the future and knows exactly what we need to become the people he has designed us to be. And he has every intention of helping us get there. So wait with your need, and wait for the answer, and while you grope through your days, envision Jesus, stopping the parade, right in front of you, loving you, longing for your healing more than you can possibly dream.

blinders off

We are all blind: blind to beauty, blind to kindness, blind to our own needs, blind to others' needs, blind to who Jesus really is. What if we all asked for sight, what if we all shouted out, "Lord! Son of David! Have mercy on me! I want to see!"?

What if we threw aside our cloaks, our comfortable though crippling covers that ward off the night? Let's fling our fears, our need to be fine, to look good or at least better—fling them off and leap to our feet in absolute trust. Let's believe that when Jesus says, "Get up," he knows what we want—we want to see—and he is absolutely merciful in answering that longing.

What do you want to see right now? Your own needs? Your own heart? The heart of Jesus? How about Jesus's face? How remarkable that this son of Precious, Valuable, gets his eyes opened and that his first glimpse of the world is of Jesus, Son of David, the very face of kindness, compassion. Mercy.

And I wonder how often when people see, really see, us, do they see Jesus?

I want to see too, Jesus: your face, your hand in this world, your touch of the miraculous. I want to see you in other people and see your compassion in me. And I want to see your kindness and mercy beam out of me, like klieg lights, on to others.

come along to...

• transfer from dark to light •

Oh, God.
I have failed so miserably at
seeing. I have turned
a blind eye to the needs around me,
I don't even recognize my own needs.
Forgive me for moving so fast
I do not have time to stop,
to halt the parade
and pay attention.
Please forgive me.
Help me, Lord,
to pay attention to my own heart,
to your heart,
and to others around me.

• transfix upon Christ •

Perhaps you will use the ancient prayer, "Christ, have mercy on me, a sinner," to move into a place of silence. Wait there, in the presence of God, and be still. Quiet your heart; your jumping, rebounding brain; your soul. If your mind wanders, just invite Jesus again: "Have mercy, Christ, have mercy." And in this place, simply love God without words.

• translate the meaning •

- *Mercy* means "compassion, kindness," shown in practical assistance, not just release from judgment, which is how we often interpret it. When have you experienced mercy? Asked for mercy? Offered it? What does it mean to you?

- Bartimaeus: "Son of Precious, son of Valuable." How would you describe yourself? "Daughter of _____" [insert a distinct, personal quality characteristic of yours like "Laughter" or "Confidence"]. Your first word may not be positive if the characteristic of your parent was a negative one, such as "Anger," but keep with it until you begin to hear the name Jesus gives you.

- How is it, asking that your needs be met? When have you been shushed for expressing your needs?

- Imagine that Jesus is asking you, "What do you want me to do for you?" How will you answer? Sit with that question, with open hands and open heart, and listen carefully to your soul's longings. Jesus stopped and the world stopped with him. There is plenty of time for healing. There is plenty of time for attentiveness. There is plenty of time to tend to your needs. Be still, in silence, and let those needs rise from a deep place within you. Take as long as you need. And then look to Jesus and raise your hands, which are full of your needs, to him.

- In what situation would you say about yourself, "I am blind. I want to see"?

• transform by renewing your mind •

Praise be to the Lord, the God of Israel, because he has come and has redeemed his people. He has raised up a horn of salvation for us in the house of his servant David..., to show mercy to our fathers and to remember his holy covenant,... to give his people the knowledge of salvation through the forgiveness of their sins, because of the tender mercy of our God, by which the rising sun will come to us from heaven to shine on those living in darkness and in the shadow of death, to guide our feet into the path of peace.

Luke 1:68–69, 72, 77–79

• transparency through prayer •

> *Dear God:*
> *You open his eyes and he sees*
> *Jesus. His first sight*
> *Is the face of your Son,*
> *Your beloved Son*
> *In whom you are so pleased.*
> *I flinch at the next part of*
> *The Story.*
> *Bartimaeus bounding off after Jesus,*
> *all innocence and wonder*
> *and wise beyond his years.*
> *He joins the parade and matches their steps and*
> *follows his Master, Savior, Healer*

To Jerusalem.
If he makes it all the way there,
How gladly he must shout, "Hosanna,"
How happily he must wave his palm branches.
What joy: he was blind, but now he sees,
And who he sees is the Messiah.
Life is a gift,
All is a gift. But he sees! He sees
And how it must destroy him,
To see, SEE, his Savior arrested,
Flogged,
Tortured, spit upon,
And hammered onto a cross for all the world to see,
To mock.
Seeing means pain
And the agony of brokenness
As we behold a dimension of the world
Once veiled to our eyes.
But seeing also means
Seeing beyond the visible
To the eternal and
Being held
In your love.
So that we too
Might invite others to see.
But the story, the blind man's story,
Our blind woman's story
Doesn't end at the cross.

Or perhaps it ends at the cross
And begins again at the empty tomb
Where you rose from the dead
And call us after you
Into life
Today
Tomorrow
And for all eternity.
Amen.

• transpired action •

How will you ask for your needs to be met today?

come along to the courtroom

Illuminations on Persistence

"Will not God bring about justice
for his chosen ones, who cry out
to him day and night?"
—LUKE 18:7

[Jesus's] point seems to be that the secret of prayer
is persistence. Keep at it, keep speaking into the
darkness, and even if nothing comes, speak again
and then again. And finally the answer is given.
It may not be the kind of answer that we want....
Instead...the answer that he gives, I think, is himself. If we go to him for anything else, he may
send us away empty or he may not. But if we go
to him for himself, I believe that we go away
always with this deepest of all our hungers filled.
—FREDERICK BUECHNER

In the movie version of Stephen King's *Rita Hayworth and the Shawshank Redemption,* Andy Dufresne, played by Tim Robbins, is imprisoned for killing his wife and her lover, and forced to serve two life sentences back to back. Eventually, his former life as a banker comes to light, and the warden moves Andy from laundry duty to the warden's office and to the library, a storage room smelling of rats and turpentine. Knowing the value of books to set prisoners free, Andy immediately begins a letter-writing campaign to the state, mailing a request for books each week for six years.

One day, an officer shoves Andy into the warden's office, where crates fill the floor and are stacked around the room. A bright grin lights his face as he rips into the cartons. He reads aloud from the accompanying instructions: "Do not write us any more letters."

Again he smiles. "Great. Now I'll write twice a week." The result, years later, is the best prison library in New England, complete with tutoring programs and GED testing and a great selection of Hank Williams. And hope.

Though most people would say, "Put up or shut up," Andy never gave up. He asked for what he needed, and kept asking. Just like the woman we will meet in our next encounter with Jesus. Come along. Pull up your mats for...

story time

The disciples cluster around Jesus, who has another story to tell, and they love his stories, love their Master's animation, the sparkle in his eyes, the drama in his voice. Half the time, maybe most of the time, they don't understand what on earth he's talking about, but they still love their story time with him.

Jesus begins:

She walks to the doorway. Tentative, frightened, but determined. She raises her hand, wads her fingers into a fist, and knocks on the doorjamb, first with a light rap, and then pounding with insistence. "Hello? Hello! Judge, I need help!"

She knows his reputation, but desperation drives her. There's no one else she can turn to, so she knocks again, thumping against the doorway, calling, calling.

The judge is someone you wouldn't send your mother to, let alone go visit yourself. He is crooked and cold-hearted. The Law ordered judges to fear God and take care of the distressed, and often imposed strict penalties on judges who failed this integrity test. This man manages to slink one step ahead of the Law and keep the shingle hanging outside. And these little old ladies he could eat for lunch. He licks his chops like the huge lion that he is.

"What do you want?"

She jumps at his growl but shoves the words through her frightened throat. It's like pushing a chain up a sand dune.

"Grant me justice against my adversary." There. The words are out. She has asked for the help she needs. She sags, nervous from exhaustion, against the door like an empty windsock, but relief does not follow this triumph.

"Don't darken my door again, lady. I don't care if you're being evicted. I don't care if everything you own is being stolen. I don't care if your children have abandoned you. I. Do. Not. Care." He separates each word, the pause in between a menace. As she peers at him through the doorway, he looks as though he might exterminate her like a bug.

"Sir. Please. Grant me justice against my adversary." Day after day she appears at his door. Twice a day, three times a day. Always the same refrain: "Please, grant me justice against my adversary."

He is a bad man, typecast perfectly for the wicked lawyer role, made fat with stiff fees and bribes. Even so, eventually he heaves a sigh, muttering to himself, "Even though I don't fear God or care about men, yet because this widow keeps bothering me, I will see that she gets justice, so that she won't eventually wear me out with her coming!"[1]

someone's knocking at the door

The widow in Jesus's story knows exactly what she needs. She is not fine, and she knows it. She also knows that she cannot stay alive if she adheres to the "don't ask for help" rule of women. Without hesitation, she occupies the main role in this parable, strong in the knowledge that the judge has to answer her, eventually, unless she dies trying to rouse his justice. She wastes no energies whining or blabbing to everyone about her misfortune or the problems with her landlord. She hauls herself and her plea directly to the one person with the power to help: the judge. She focuses her resources on solving the problem. Her face must be radiant with determination, knowing in her soul that right makes might.

She has a heart for justice, so she is able to persist in pounding on his door, seeking that right. She clearly understands her own worth and the judge's role in protecting that worth. She is alone. No husband fights her cause. No children shelter her. No one takes up the gauntlet in her name, on her behalf. She cannot rely on anyone, except herself and her own desperation, and, unfortunately, the lazy and wicked judge.

In ancient times, widows were the marginalized of society. Along with infants, they were the most vulnerable of God's children. We see God's care for the widow of Zarephath (1 Kings 17:7–24), of Ruth and Naomi, both widows. Jesus commended a widow's faith as he watched her put all she owned into the offering box (see Luke 21:2). Strict laws and ordinances required provisions for protection and sustenance of widows. "Do not take advantage of a widow or an orphan" (Exodus 22:22). "[God] defends the cause of the fatherless and the widow, and loves the alien, giving him food and clothing" (Deuteronomy 10:18).

The example of the New Testament church makes clear the importance of caring for widows (see 1 Timothy 5:3–16). "This is pure and undefiled religion in the sight of our God and Father, to visit orphans and widows in their distress" (James 1:27, NASB).

This feels good. Great, actually, until the only person between the widow, homelessness, and certain starvation is a judge who left his heart in San Francisco. This widow is dependent on the judge to do right, even if he isn't a good judge. We have to commend her for such determination. She not only asks for help, she demands that he help her.

This is not my way. I pout, whine, sulk, withdraw. I absent myself, try to become invisible, raise my voice, descend to ugliness to get what I want. I pretend, I invite mind reading—no, I expect mind reading. I worry, wring my hands, journal, moan, and try whining some more. I isolate, slam, stomp, and make any scene possible to achieve my ends.

I think I've found a better role model than the fishwife I've been. Oh, that I might have the persistence of this almost-destitute widow when it comes to asking for my legitimate needs to be met.

But the language of desire, of needs, is a language that we do not easily speak. Nor do we accommodate well, in our crammed, chaotic, frantic lifestyles, the basic meeting of our own needs. We expend much energy meeting or attempting to meet others' needs, even sacrificing basic self-care in order to tend to them, so much so that many women no longer know who they are—if they ever knew in the first place. This neglect of our needs is a kind of blindness on our part, and until we begin to ask ourselves, "What do I need?" I don't see us getting better anytime soon. But James said, "You do not have because you do not ask" (4:2, NASB), so we learn to ask. We knock, we seek, and we keep asking, seeking, knocking, even if the judge isn't answering the door.

judge—not?

So there is nothing positive to say about the judge in Jesus's story, other than he finally gave in to good, to the right thing, but only because otherwise she would never leave him alone. The literal translation of "so that she won't eventually wear me out with her coming!" is "lest she come at last and beat me."[2] Rather than a rolling pin from classic comics, this widow brandishes righteousness with never-give-up character. "You will meet my needs because it is the right thing to do, because it is your *job*, because it is the Law."

Strict laws and severe punishment aside,[3] it's not fear of penalty that wins over this judge. He doesn't fear God or care about people. No, the woman's persistence finally persuades him to use his might to make right happen. "Because this widow keeps bothering me, I will see that she gets justice," he concludes. It's brave of Jesus to use such a hideous judge to stand in for God in the story, because it's so far from a true picture of God—God is holy and just, and this judge just the opposite: wicked, lazy. The truth is, we can't compare this judge and God at all.

But perhaps Jesus knows that many people see God as just such a heartless and cruel judge. Perhaps that's why the caricature. Because if the wicked and lazy judge will eventually, after much badgering, do the right thing, then how much more will God, the true God, the God of justice and Lord of all the earth, the God who loves you more than all the earth, do justly? So, because of who God is, we persist in asking for what we need, despite a seeming lack of answers. You may not get your answer immediately, but don't stop asking, because God—who has the long view of the situation—will act justly. As Abraham asked in Genesis 18:25, "Will not the Judge of all the earth do right?"

Meanwhile, as we wait, what are we to learn from unanswered prayers, from the persistent, insistent heartfelt cries that go without response, seeming to fall on deaf ears?

the myth of unanswered prayer

I'm not sure there is any such thing as unanswered prayer. I think God always answers, but when we don't get the answer we want, we figure he's zipped his lips and gone hunting, turned his back on us. Sometimes the answers are wrapped in situations that don't seem to be answers at all, but somehow serve to hasten God's plan.

For instance, when my husband and I moved into missionary calling and relinquished the car provided for my husband through the pastorate, I believed that on the right day God would show up with keys in his hands, knock on our door, and hand over a title. I really did believe this. It happened to a friend of mine, and her husband wasn't even a pastor. Why couldn't it happen to us?

Instead, God provided a neighbor and friend, Amy, who volunteered to share her van with us. We labored over our calendars, compared lists of needs and duties, and I made it to every single speaking engagement on my schedule, thanks to her.

And then, *mamma mia*! and *oy vey*! our children needed braces. I thought I would throw up at this news, and yet, in straight-toothed, movie-star America, we can't bear the thought of our children running around all snaggletoothed. So off we trundled, praying for a favorable long-term payment plan, to a doctor I found after pulling exactly one question out of my crowded mind and life: how long will it take me to get to your office?

This orthodontist, it turned out, had a heart for pastors, and when he learned that my husband is a pastor and that we are missionaries, he provided free orthodontia. *Free.* For three children. And their mother.

So while I was waiting for a car, God was all busy, getting ready to give my whole family smiles that would last a lifetime, bring light to others, and gleam at God's goodness.

responding to no

Sometimes, of course, the answer is just plain no. I may think I need a particular job, or my child needs a particular favor, or my husband needs a particular something or other. But God tells us, kindly, "'For my thoughts are not your thoughts, neither are your ways my ways,' declares the LORD. 'As the heavens are higher than the earth, so are my ways higher than your ways and my thoughts than your thoughts'" (Isaiah 55:8–9).

Those are the times I want to sing the jingle, "My dad's bigger than your dad…" only with the words, "My idea's better than your idea, God," because all I can see is my own agenda.

But perhaps God's agenda is, "wait." Timing is everything to this compassionate and just God, who lives outside of time. When events unfurl like a flag, we see exactly what he was up to while we waited and accused him of not caring or of procrastinating. We must believe that behind a seeming no is a much better plan than we could ask or imagine (see Ephesians 3:20).

So how to respond in the meantime?

One friend, Claudia, met her diagnosis of cancer with high faith. Her family rallied around her, and her hopes were vibrant, though the cancer markers indicated problems. She was not being healed of cancer, but God was healing her marriage; bringing her family into a closer-knit, faith-filled center; moving her husband back to faith. Intermittent miracles have brought great joy and increased the faith of those who love her. There is, written in the story of her life, a quiet faith in this inscrutable God, who will act justly though perhaps not in the way she had hoped.

She continues to engage in life and relationships with joy, even in the midst of God's "not right now, maybe never" answer. Seeing her with her grandbabies, or circulating through her family's business, or gathering flowers from her garden, I am struck with the peace on her beautiful face, the certainty of her gifted hands, the kindness of her presence. And as her friends have fought for her, accompanying her to doctors' offices, sitting with her during treatments, railing against heaven on her behalf, they are the richer for it. They cheer when the markers are low. They weep together when hot spots appear. They hold fast in prayer for their friend. They are learning to see, in God's "no, not now, maybe not ever," an even better yes.

And then, no matter what, everyone wins.

persistence pays off

Because she persists, the door-pounding widow finally gets her plea answered, finding resolution for her distress. What do we learn as we hold the course, praying repeatedly, seeking answers we do not receive?

Growth.

The delay may increase our passion for the subject of the prayer. Our earnestness and care for a loved one, or for some immense need, will grow as we continue to seek God on behalf of our prayer focus. As we pray, as we seek God's help, as we bow to God's authority in our lives and in the lives of people we love, our hearts grow too. As we keep laying our hearts out for God, baring our souls with our deep needs and heartbreak, our belief in God's sovereignty will flourish. As we persist in prayer, our trust levels will rise, and we will live lighter, even though "no" and "wait" seem to be the answers for the hour, day, week, year, decade.

Our motives become clearer as we continue to seek God. Why do we want this so badly? Is God pleased with our hearts as we pound on heaven's lintels? Are we desperate for God, or for God's answers? Sometimes I wonder if God tarries in answering so that we will be desperate for God as well as earnest about our desires.

And as we persist in prayer, in faithfulness, earnestly longing for what we cannot see, God increases our faith: the longer we pray, the more certain we are that God, only God, can do justly.

but God, i'm so tired...

What keeps us from persisting, from holding fast to what we know we can ask for, even though heaven seems silent as a cemetery?

- **Weariness:** Sometimes we are just plain tired. Our troubles pile up on us like a freight-train wreck, and usurp the place of God's Word, of prayer, of real rest. Reevaluate your soul care during this time. If you are in distress, under duress, you need your rest.

- **Lack of focus:** Oh, I get so distracted with life and craziness that I forget to ask, that I start running amuck, like iron shavings without a magnet. Stillness helps me focus, silence brings rest to my popping-corn brain and takes me back to my heart, and God's, where I can invite him to speak and clarify my needs and heartaches and pains.

- **Discouragement and doubt:** "Maybe I don't really need this," or, "I'm not supposed to pray for this," or, "I'm doing it all wrong," or, "Maybe God isn't really a good God and doesn't really care…" Don't be surprised if these thoughts flit across your soul like a shadow, or if they land on the telephone wire above your heart and screech out their mocking cries like ugly crows. The Enemy loves to caw doubt in our hearts: doubt that we are deserving of God's attention, doubt that we have any right to ask so much, doubt that God really loves us. Don't let that mockingbird land. Shoo him away and run back to God. God understands your doubts and discouragement, and will quickly gather you in his arms and soothe you.

holding the course

Who knows how long that road to answered prayer might be? If you feel like you've signed up for the Forrest Gump School of Long-Distance Running, don't stop. There are ways to stay faithful, persistent like the widow, continuing to ask God for what you need.

We hold on to what we know: We know that we are not supposed to do this alone. We know that God is just and holy, and will always act in our best interests. God is always for us, though answers may seem slow in coming.

Review what is true about God, how he is compassionate, abounding in love, slow to anger. Recite that truth, as Jesus said in Luke 18:7–8: "And will not God bring about justice for his chosen ones, who cry out to him day and night? Will he keep putting them off? I tell you, he will see that they get justice, and quickly." And remember, God gets to define "quickly."

Today, as I waited before God, my heart full of unanswered pleas for people I love, desperate with longing to see answers, I chose to speak, out loud, the truth about God. And before I was five words into listing God's character traits, tears began to pour. Yes, for the people I love. But even more, for the God I love, who will always do justly.

God's watch reads differently than our timepiece, and we must constantly resync our souls with God's timing.

On long journeys, it's good to have traveling companions. But we keep our pain and our pleas under wraps much of the time. Why are you carrying this alone? Can you invite just one trusted person into the prayer place with you; can you ask just one person to help bear this burden? When your candle burns low and sputters in the melted wax of disappointment and sorrow and pain, surround yourself with people who will bring the light, pray, be a relay partner in the race. Sometimes, though, our prayer need is so private, so deep, that we feel unable to share it with others, and maybe self-protection is necessary. Even so, especially in those times, rally friends to pray for unspecified struggles, so that you are not alone. And when you cannot bang on the doorpost one more time, relinquish your burden to another who promises to carry it for you before God, while you rest.

Please, please, please hold the course! We will be able to say with grins as big and bright as a half moon and with thanksgiving to God, along with Paul, "I have fought the good fight, I have finished the race, I have kept the faith" (2 Timothy 4:7).

the widowed soul

Whether you are married or not, perhaps you too have felt like a widow:

- spiritually alone in your marriage or singleness
- disrespected because of poverty or failure or lostness or misfortune
- weary of your sole and solo responsibilities for your life and being
- helpless with no one to advocate for you

Hear God's words: "Come to me. You are of such great worth to me. I love the sparrows, I love the lilies of the field…how much more do I love you? And how much more just and caring am I than those for whom your heart longs?" (see Matthew 6:26–28; 10:29–31).

And what about that landlord? Who is your landlord, the person in your life or acquaintance or past who simply doesn't care, whose heart is as hard as a new saddle and as cold as a corpse? Who hasn't loved you well, hasn't tended to your heart's cry, hasn't shown compassion for your needs or has minimized them? That person is not your final jury. That person does not deliver the verdict. Because you can appeal to the real Judge.

Ask for what you need. God wants to hear, waits to help. God is abundant in mercy and abounding in loving-kindness. Ask, and keep asking, always inviting the Lord of all the earth to do justly. And to clarify your vision, purify your desires, intensify your passion. To change you. Then, no matter what, you win. The good Judge will deal justly.

Headings in my older Bibles describe the woman in Jesus's

story as "The Importunate Widow." I love that word: *importunate*. Such an unfailing, headlong word for such a strong woman in such a weak position in society. And yet her very desperation, her weakness, propelled her forward, forcing her into the awkward position of insistent beggar, persistent in her pleas, her begging bowl always before her. Her position became her gift and brought forth a strength she'd never needed in the past and perhaps didn't even realize existed.

So it is with our rock-hard spaces, those times in our lives when all of our begging pushes us not only to our knees but to our Savior. And there, knowing that we are destitute without him, incapable of moving forward, we receive his strength to prevail.

Unlike the widow, no one can evict you from your true Home. And when the Son of Man comes, he will find faith on this earth.

Honestly. It's enough to make you beam.

come along to...

 • transfer from dark to light •

Dear God,
Here I am.
I have asked for what I wanted—
But asked with wrong motives.
Or I failed to ask, or just dropped out of the battle.
I confess that doubt and discouragement sometimes win
The battle for my soul.

Please forgive me for failing to run,
For trying to run alone,
For forgetting that you are God
No matter what the answer may be.
I want to learn to live in your
Yes, your No, your Wait and See
With peace and joy.
I want to be radiant with your
Hope.
Thank you that in Christ
All things are possible.
Please pick up my heart
Once again.

• transfix upon Christ •

Still your frenetically beating heart. Wait. Turn your mind to God. Shush the wailing, fretful frightened child you feel like, and just be still. As worries arise, hold them out to God and move back to stillness. Love God there, and let God love you. Breathe deeply. Let that love fill your lungs and run through your body like oxygen.

• translate the meaning •

• In what ways do you feel widowed? When have you consistently banged on heaven's door for help in a hard place? What wearies you in your persistence? Where is there discouragement, doubt, lack of focus?

- Where do you waste energy and lose direction by whining, complaining, blabbing to others?
- Who is the landlord in your life, the absentee person who cares nothing for your well-being? How do you take this person to God? How do you sidestep this roadblock and keep moving to God?
- Who runs alongside you and sometimes even spells you in the race? If no one, why is that? Who can you invite to share this journey with you?
- How can you move to a place where you can treasure God's no as much as you treasure God's yes? What stands in the way of that faith movement?

• transform by renewing your mind •

Ask and it will be given to you; seek and you will find; knock and the door will be opened to you. For everyone who asks receives; he who seeks finds; and to him who knocks, the door will be opened.

Matthew 7:7–8

• transparency through prayer •

Father God:
You are the righteous Judge.
But I am tired of begging and pleading
And I am not certain I am even asking aright anymore.
Please interpret my heart's groans
And do your will in the long-distance burden

I carry.
I trust you, and lay down my load at your feet.
And here I find the freedom
I seek:
Absolute trust that you will act rightly
In my life
And in the lives of people I love.
I count on it.
And I am so grateful.
Thank you.
In the name of Jesus, the one who said,
"Ask,"
Amen.

• transpired action •

How will you ask for what you need, without giving up, today?

come along
to the crowd

Illuminations on Healing

"Daughter.... Go in peace and be freed
from your suffering."
—MARK 5:34

Tell God all that is in your heart, as one unloads
one's heart, its pleasures and its pains, to a dear
friend. Tell him your troubles, that he may
comfort you; tell him your joys, that he may
sober them; tell him your longings, that he may
purify them; tell him your dislikes, that he may
help you conquer them; talk to him of your
temptations, that he may shield you from them:
show him the wounds of your heart, that he
may heal them.... If you thus pour out all your
weaknesses, needs, troubles, there will be no lack

> of what to say.... Talk out of the abundance of
> [the] heart, without consideration...say just
> what [you] think. Blessed are they who attain to
> such familiar, unreserved intercourse with God.
> —François Fénelon

In the film *When a Man Loves a Woman*, Meg Ryan plays Alice Green, a loving and sexy wife and mother...and an alcoholic who drinks a quart of vodka by 10:00 a.m. She is a funny, cute, charming drunk, until she nearly destroys her children and ruins her marriage. After working hard at rehab, and staying sober, and attending meetings, she still has no marriage. She tells her story at an open Alcoholics Anonymous meeting.

"It's horrifying how much you can hate yourself for being low and weak, and [my husband] couldn't save me from that. So I turned it on him. I tried to empty it onto him. But there was always more, you know. When he tried to help, I told him that he made me feel small and worthless. But nobody makes us feel that, we do that for ourselves. I shut him out because I knew if he ever really saw who I was inside, that he wouldn't love me. And we're separated now. He's moved away, and it was so hard not to beg him to stay. And I don't know if I'm going to get a second chance, but I have to believe that I deserve one because we all do."[1]

Telling the story not only cemented Alice's own healing; telling her story began the long healing necessary for their marriage. When Alice owned her past, though her past impacted all her relationships, she began to propel herself toward a better future.

We all have problems, but help may be just a touch away.

Come along, and sneak a peek into the life of a woman who received what she hadn't even dreamed of seeking.

alone in a crowd

Hordes surround Jesus. It's worse than a rock concert! Hands reach out, press against him, leaving needy fingerprints everywhere. People are desperate to touch this miracle man, this wondrous worker who showed up in society from nowhere and started healing people right and left.

No one notices the woman, alone. She guards a bubble of space about her, with her shoulders drawn forward, her body curled over like the fronds of a weeping cherry tree. Her skin is thin as rice paper, her face lined from years of isolation and illness. Pain haunts her eyes, and something more. Loneliness. She is a hollow shell of a woman, like half of a scooped-out gourd, and she knows only one thing: in the waves of crushing humanity, she must reach Jesus—he is the one who can heal her.

But after more than a decade of shame, of aloneness, of being considered unclean, she wants only to be lost in the crowd, anonymous in the melee of seekers.

She approaches Jesus from behind, raises her hand to tap him on the shoulder, then pulls herself back. She dare not touch this holy man.

What choices remain? For twelve years she sought the advice of every doctor around, from bushman quack to bona fide medic. No one, not one single person, had a solution. They had ideas, but no cure. Now, after the endless indignities from the doctors, after the shame and humiliation, she is penniless, her money lining their pockets, and has nothing to show for all her seeking.

Her bleeding continued. So did her social stigma. She lost her friends. Since neither God nor doctor had thus far deigned to heal her, her faith whittled down to a stub. Her symptoms increased: loss of energy due to anemia, poor posture from holding her cramping abdomen or lying doubled over with pain from her unending menses. Chronic illness and this solitary confinement merge into one long, dark depression. Her energy levels scrape bottom daily.

But now, all these years later, she hears at last of someone—Someone—who might hold the healing touch. After all, no one has ever seen healings like he performs (see Luke 8:43–48).[2]

unclean, unclean

Touch, however, for this woman, in this time, is a problem. Jesus could be considered unclean as well, because of her bleeding. According to the Law, a woman on her menstrual period is unclean for a week. Meanwhile, during that time, everything that even her clothing touches is unclean, anything she sits upon is unclean, and anyone touching these items is unclean. Further, for unnatural blood flow, the woman is unclean for the entire time of the flow; that means a dozen long years for this woman. Presumably being in a crowd causes concern, because contact with anyone her garments touch means uncleanness for the other (see Leviticus 15:19–33).

This plays havoc with this woman's love life too. Anyone having sexual contact with a woman during her period would be cut off from the people of Israel (see Leviticus 20:18). Twelve years is a long time for a husband to go without intimate touch with his wife. So commentators assume that this woman, if she was once a wife, is no longer married, that her marriage dissolved as a result of her constant hemorrhaging.

Sometimes relationships do dissolve because of crisis. Chronic illness, loss of a child, catastrophe—any of these things can wedge in between loved ones. The anguish and stress of holding on in the midst of such hardship is sometimes too much.

On another level, relationships get messed up because we are, well, let's face it: we are a bloodied people, a mess, and sometimes we hurt others. While our messiness may impact others, creating pain, shame, and anger, we cannot carry the blame for their reactions to those feelings after we repent. In other words, if they choose to remain in pain or unforgiveness when we have sought forgiveness for hurt we inflicted, if they choose to revert to shame after we have tried to sort out the problem with them, if they choose to cling to anger rather than to the healing Jesus offers, then we have to release the problem. Our own sorrow over our sin, when it leads to repentance, is fully cleansed by Christ, and the circle is completed when we seek reconciliation with the one against whom we sinned.

If they choose to keep us at an "unclean" distance, then all we can do is what Jesus said: "Love the Lord your God with all your heart...soul...mind and...strength" (Mark 12:30). We move on with the relationship as though forgiveness has occurred, for we have truly received it from Christ.

no mess allowed

So one hundred and forty-four times the moon passes through its cycles—an eternity for a woman to be so touch-deprived, a lifetime to be bleeding. Even her skin must ache from the lack of intimacy and affection. All this makes for one lonely woman. The loneliness accumulates, and surely the isolation eats away at her, just as anemia and fatigue must combine into a deadly potion of discouragement. But desperation drives her, forcing her out among the people. What courage it takes for her to risk, one more time, the possibility and disappointment of nonhealing.

Her single-minded search impresses me. She continues to hunt down healing. Her world shrinks to one focal point, life with a zoom lens: finding a cure for the bleeding. She knows that recovery is possible, and she refuses to suspend the search.

Sometimes we never even start. Somehow we swallowed the bitter pill of belief that demanded, "Don't have problems. And if you do, don't talk about them with anyone else." We live under a false, do-good slogan: altruism preferred over health.

I don't think this is why Jesus came, so that we could volunteer ourselves to death, perfect-woman-wife-and-mother ourselves toward the mortuary.

A therapist friend says, "Recovery comes first." That means recovery before your schooling, before your advancement at work, before your redecorating project or garden upheaval plans or concocting your next vacation or upgrading your computer. What will it take to get well, to seek healing, to mend emotionally, spiritually? When will you start? How will you dodge your shadow-boxing opponent, discouragement? The importunate widow never quit—she wearied the judge with her constant badgering until he indulged in some real ethics and helped her. This woman, with her exhausting blood flow, never quits either.

Let's take down the No Messies Allowed sign and reach for the healing each of us needs.

losing yourself

I think about the hemorrhaging woman's twelve-year trauma. Twelve years really isn't too bad, when I consider how long it took me to start looking for help, and then to stop looking in the wrong places: losing myself in fiction, or in isolation or anger, or rushing and constant activity: these kept me fishing in puddles on the concrete and wondering why I wasn't catching fish.

There are so many reasons, aren't there, why we might not seek healing?

Maybe you don't want to bother anyone. *Don't make a big deal out of this, okay?* you think. You don't want anyone to believe the worst of you because you aren't "well"—how the world would define "well"—in the first place, and though we know that Jesus came for the sick rather than the healthy, we also know that people around us sure seem pretty healthy on the surface.

Plus, the Anonymity Factor enters the equation. Just as the hemorrhaging woman crept up behind Jesus, so do we try to keep our "stuff" secret, hoping no will notice our spiritual anemia, the eternal emotional bloodletting. We creep around, glancing about for help in our few seconds of spare time but not making it a primary focus each day. We think, *If I pay too much attention, maybe the problems will be worse than I thought.* Or, *I really won't ever find help, the right help, resources.* Or, *People will consider me vain and self-centered. I have to push past the crowd that is more comfortable when I don't need anything; when I do, then I shouldn't make noise about it. People might think me selfish. It's safer to play down my deepest longings and gut it out. Or quit when pursuing healing becomes inconvenient, or when my messiness threatens to become too public.*

But when the excuses settle and the not-healing drapes over us and our loved ones like dust covering an abandoned vacation cottage, we realize the truth. We have let pride get in the way. We've too proudly thought we shouldn't ask for help, shouldn't have needs.

That is such a lie. No matter what our interests or obligations: Healing comes first. Recovery is the first priority…because if you are hemorrhaging in your soul, you are dying, and then who wins?

Do more than stanch the flow. Get real help, like our woman sandwiched in with the multitude surrounding Jesus. The crowd pushes between her and Jesus. The woman slips, like the shadow she has become, between the shouting, shoving people. And, so light no one would notice, like a dust mote, she touches the fringe on his garment.[3]

Faster than a heartbeat, her bleeding ceases. She knows deep within that her body is healed. Touching Jesus's clothes set her free. Didn't her hand tremble when she touched the cloth like a butterfly on his shoulder, tremble from the power he emitted, the healing in his wings?

Before she can react, Jesus swings around. "Who touched my clothes?"

Alarm and awe strike her silent. She freezes in place. The disciples hurtle into the verbal void. "You see the people crowding against you…yet you can ask, 'Who touched me?'" (see Mark 5:30–31).

The woman drags air into her lungs, starting to breathe again. But Jesus keeps looking, searching the crowd for the face. *For her face.*

"Someone touched me; I know that power has gone out from me."

She falls at his feet, the adrenaline of fear rushing through her body. The words tremble from her, the whole humiliating story tumbling from her lips. The bleeding, the doctors, the desperation, the isolation, the telltale touch.

our stories

Sometimes we absolutely must tell our stories in order for healing to be complete. The hemorrhaging woman's body was healed when she touched Jesus's garment, but what about her heart?

In *The Last Sin Eater* by Francine Rivers, after generations of sin and broken relationships in a particular mountain valley, healing begins for individuals and the community as people tell their stories. A lovely woman, who had lived in isolation on Dead Man's

Mountain, explains her father's abuse of her mother, her mother's desperation and suicide, the father's subsequent sexual abuse of herself, her father's death, her own love and loss.[4] She found forgiveness and grace through Jesus Christ, but the corporate healing and the healing of her heart in community begin when she stands and tells her story to the people gathered before her.

This is an important gift of women's retreats, and one of my favorite times: when I can sit with women and listen to their stories. Not their favorite chicken recipe, although I am happy to try a new dish (especially a tightwad one), but the ingredients that make up their lives thus far. *Where have you come from; what was your family like, your parents, your home life; how is your heart these days; where is there pain, joy; what do you look forward to?* Oh, what a privilege for us to share these stories of our lives and invite others into the gift of accepting us, all composite and collage, cheap metals mixed in with the pure gold that brings a lovely sheen to each of our souls.

But this goes against the grain of our culture, doesn't it? Our culture says, "Don't wear your heart on your sleeve." "Don't tell your troubles to others." "Put on a happy face." And so telling our stories is like inviting company over and not cleaning the house, but rather showing them the junk pitched down the basement stairs and hidden in the dishwasher or stuffed with the dust bunnies under the bed; it's like giving a tour of the crawlspace, or even the compost pile.

How interesting, then, that a colloquialism we use for this social process of telling our stories is "coming clean." It really does help to reverse the "unclean, unclean" feeling of being a woman who is hemorrhaging, a woman who bears wounds, a woman who is messy.

Even if the story pours forth like a hemorrhage of words, what story do you need to tell? To whom will you tell it? Find a safe recipient. Practice by telling Jesus your story: Where you have been? How have you responded or reacted to life? Where are you bleeding? Tell him where you've looked for answers, where you've spent or misspent your energies.

Then take in the rest of the story.

daughter

"Who touched me?" Jesus asks. I love this—this man who can read minds and knows people's hearts asks the crowd, "Who touched me?" Of course he knows who touched him, but perhaps her healing is not yet complete. He asks her to go public with her story, for her own sake. The gift of telling her story is immense for a woman riddled with loneliness, weak from her losses, weary with her search for healing.

But Jesus still has one more gift to impart. He looks the woman full in the eyes, listens with love to her story, and says the un-believable: "Daughter."

Did Jesus really call her "daughter"?

Hear the gift in that word. This woman, who has been alone for so long, despised for so long, untouched for so long, is being called such an affectionate term. Touching his garment unchains her body. And when that word touches her—*daughter*—her soul begins to mend. She is claimed into the very family of this man sent from God. "Daughter, your faith has healed you. Go in peace and be freed from your suffering" (Mark 5:34). She who has been abandoned by medical doctors and ostracized from others is restored to relationship with her people and her God. She may not be a mother. She may not be a wife. We don't know. But we do know that she was once someone's daughter.

Her story is our story. You may not carry these other roles of femininity—wife or mother—but you are a daughter too. As a daughter, you've experienced all the ups and downs, the goodness and harshness of being part of a family circle. Perhaps you don't even know your parents because the relationship was severed years ago. Or you don't know them well because sometimes families can be aloof from one another. We each bring our own wounds into relationships, even those relationships that are supposed to be for good and not for harm. And so maybe your inventory shows some abandonment wounds, or some sorrow over the lack of family you had, or wish you had, growing up: your parents did not love you the way you needed and deserved to be loved. Your family has let you down in all their fallen humanity. Or you have let them down, not been the daughter or family member you meant to be. Likely both ring true. You've failed in your familial roles, and in your friendships. This can become its own bondage, rendering you anemic. Or you create a bubble around yourself in order to protect yourself—or others—and the isolation eats away at you until depression forms a barnacle-like suction on your soul.

So when Jesus calls the woman with the heavy flow of blood "Daughter," he claims her into his family. He claims his own authority over that family, and his own ability to heal and pronounce freedom. And in naming her, Jesus places her, once again, in the lovely position of dependency and the care-less freedom of knowing that someone will see to her needs, just as a parent would in a healthy home. With his word, he invites her home again, and he invites us home too.

"Daughter, your faith has healed you. Go in peace and be freed from your suffering" (Mark 5:34).

You have to love Jesus all the more for the rest of his sentence. Not only does he affirm the hemorrhaging woman's faith, but he also wipes out her anxiety. "Go in peace." A new path for this woman, whose feet have trod only the road of loneliness and illness.

Peace.

Jesus has rerouted her life.

How fascinating that Jesus says, "Be freed from your suffering." The Scriptures have already told us, "Immediately her bleeding stopped and she felt in her body that she was freed from her suffering" (verse 29). Perhaps Jesus pronounced not just freedom from the illness, the severe bleeding of a dozen years, but much more. Perhaps he was announcing to the woman and to all around them that the healing is larger, that we can be freed from the effects of suffering—the loss of energy and relationships, the loss of blood and joy, the loss of faith and hope.

This is more miraculous than the woman in the story dared to hope, more than she could ask or imagine. This is Jesus, reiterating the healing of a woman beyond hope, and this is Jesus offering the same to me and you: a healing beyond hope.

Can you hear his words? "Daughter, your faith has healed you. Go in peace and be freed from your suffering." Let him meet your eyes and say this to you, over and over. Listen. Believe. Dare to reach for his sleeve. Invite him to set you free from your suffering, to descend on you in peace and lead you forward, a daughter once again.

come along to...

 • transfer from dark to light •

Dear God,
I have dragged my suffering with me
From pillar to post
And back again
And today
I confess my sin.
You have promised to heal my heart
Even if my "bleeding" never stops
And I have chosen to nurse my pain
And the effects of my suffering
And not walk in peace.
Please forgive me.
And please,
Please set me free
From my suffering
And reroute my path.

• transfix upon Christ •

Peace. Freed from suffering. Imagine how she felt to be embraced by this man's words, his eye contact, his healing. Be still in Christ's presence. Hold up before him your wounds, your bleeding, your losses. And then be still. Rest.

• translate the meaning •

- When have you felt alone in a crowd, bubble-wrapped by your pain, isolated by suffering? How did you reach out for help? What areas now keep you from transparency with others?
- Where have you experienced forgiveness and then, when confessing your sin to another, found that they would not release their own pain? How do you keep loving in that position?
- Consider your family relationships, your disappointments and pain from living with imperfect people. From being an imperfect person yourself in those relationships. What hinders your healing now?
- The woman with the hemorrhage refused to give up her search for healing. If recovery comes first, what steps do you need to take to begin the process? What stops you from starting?
- Jesus said, "Daughter.… Go in peace and be freed from your suffering." What might you need to relinquish in order to experience that peace and freedom?

• transform by renewing your mind •

Do not fear, for I am with you; do not anxiously look about you,
for I am your God. I will strengthen you, surely I will help you,
Surely I will uphold you with My righteous right hand.

Isaiah 41:10, NASB

• transparency through prayer •

Dear God,
I am tired. I am tired of "bleeding,"
Weary with my losses:
Of friends, family, faith.
Weary at what life has cost me,
And tired of the nonhealing.
But I turn to you now.
I reach for the fringe of your cloak,
And then I hear your word:
You call me "Daughter,"
And by that name, I know you are calling me
Back into your protective arms,
Your loving embrace,
Your kindness.
And your healing.
May your power go out from you
And into me.
Set me on the path of peace,

And free me from my suffering.
In Jesus's name,
Amen.

• transpired action •

How will you practice being honest about your problems, and telling your story?

come along to the party

Illuminations on the Fragrance of Gratitude

"Your sins are forgiven."
—LUKE 7:48

O gracious Light, Pure brightness of the everlasting
Father in heaven, O Jesus Christ, holy and
blessed!

> Now as we come to the setting of the sun,
> And our eyes behold the vesper light
> We sing praises, O God: Father, Son and Holy

Spirit.

> You are worthy at all times to be praised by

happy voices,

> O Son of God, O giver of life,
> And to be glorified through all the worlds.
> —"Phos Hilaron" ("Song of the Light")

They were not the lovely people in our long-ago church. With teeth missing, and lank hair, they wore the same permanently stained and mismatched clothes day after day. He always insisted on a hug, on touching, and people wanted to run from him. Many did.

But not Jesus.

They found Jesus, or rather, Jesus found them.

When I last saw this couple from a far distant time in our lives, their teeth were still broken or absent, their hair still lifeless. When I saw them coming, I prayed. I am embarrassed to say that I had to pray to see Jesus in them, and not pretend to be occupied and thus avoid contact. They were so kind, so friendly, wanting to know how big our kids are now, how is Rich, how am I?

I watched them, and every time the husband spoke, his wife looked at him with adoring eyes and the utmost respect. *They are radiant together,* I realized, *just glowing.*

I had forgotten how every single conversation with this couple turned to Jesus.

"I just can't believe Jesus loves a sinner like me," he said, voice hushed as though in a recording studio. "I can't believe it. I don't deserve his love."

I looked at him, with his mismatched and soiled clothes, and felt shame scuttle up the trellis of my heart. Oh, they deserve Jesus's love so much more than I. They, with no artifice, just know they need him, and they love him with huge, open hearts. I, on the other hand, wage a constant battle between measuring up to my own expectations, and repenting and needing Jesus.

This couple will win no popularity contests on earth. They won't be invited to the big soirees and housewarmings. But they will hear Jesus's "Well done" one day. Because their relationship with him makes waves. They rock the boat of people's expectations and judgments to follow Christ.

When I bow my heart before God, I see them, and I ask that God would help me to make waves too, just like they do.

Come along, Jesus reminds me, and see how to do this. Crash a party and meet a woman radically loved, radically forgiven, who loved radically in return.

a waterfall

Polite society won't meet her eyes, yet still she runs through the streets, arms laden with her treasure. She reaches the door and leans on the doorjamb, gasping for air. "Is the Teacher here?" she asks, gulping around the question (see Luke 7:36–50).

The servant stares at her, eyes appraising.

She raises her chin, straightens her back, meets his gaze straight on.

He stands aside and she presses past him, heading toward the sound of voices, laughter.

At the doorway, she stops. Her heart pounds, but not from the run. Something else. With his back to her, the Teacher reclines at the table, so casual, friendly, warm in tone with the other important guests. As a party crasher and a woman, she is supposed to stay away from the center of the activity, to listen from the sidelines, to be invisible—welcome, in theory, but invisible. A laugh, an old laugh, rasps past her lips, and is gone. Invisible no more, she is through with pretending to be a less-than citizen, or no citizen at all, worse than the dogs. She is through with the judgment, the censuring eyes, the burning familiarity beneath some of the men's gazes. She is through with the resentment that accompanies her every step.

She is a different woman than these people know. Her heart fills up with gratitude, and her throat tightens. Before she can talk herself back from the brink, her tears spill out. She finds herself near his feet, and she falls to her knees, a waterfall pouring from the buried stream of her heart. She places her heavy burden on the floor to free her hands, to wipe her cheeks. How long since she has cried? Ten years? Twenty? Has she ever wept like this, for this reason?

No, never. Realizing this triggers such an outpouring of tears that Jesus's feet are wet. With no cloth, she unbinds her long hair and dries his feet with the thick curtain. She kisses his feet, those feet that carry such good news to the likes of her.

And then, with one fast *thunk,* she breaks the neck of the bottle. The thick, cloudy jar tips, and the room fills with the fragrance spilling over Jesus's feet.

the life of the party?

By now, Jesus is no longer the center of attention. All conversation halts. Everyone observes her every move, various expressions flitting across and then lodging on their faces: surprise, judgment, recognition, shame, anger. Across the room, arms folded across his chest, the host watches her, eyes narrowed. Appropriately named Simon, which means "obedient one,"[1] and as a Pharisee, his obedience is a source of great pride.

"If this man were a prophet, he would know who is touching him and what kind of woman she is—that she is a sinner." To even wonder about his guest's "prophet" status would shock the dinner companions. He keeps his judgment to himself, ever the proper host. So at Jesus's words, he jerks in surprise.

Because Jesus answers him—his very thoughts! "Simon, I have something to tell you."

What can Simon say? He brought the Teacher here so they could all listen to him. "Tell me, teacher." His puffs his chest at the attention, but inside, doubt worms its way to his underutilized heart.

The Rabbi is known for his stories. The audience looks at him, rapt, and Simon tries to paste the same expression on his own face. But his heart beats the complicated rhythm of fear...or is it doom?

"Two men owed money to a moneylender. One owed five hundred silver coins, about five hundred days' wages. The other owed fifty. Neither of them had the money to pay the moneylender back, so the lender canceled both debts." Jesus pauses.

Simon raises his gaze to Jesus's face, stopping somewhere around the bridge of his nose. Eye contact is becoming harder.

"Now which one do you think will love the moneylender more?"

Two months versus twenty months? A no-brainer, an answer-in-your-sleep question, but Simon worries it about like a fish nipping at a worm. There's a trick in there, but he can't figure out what it is. He forces the answer past clenched teeth: "I suppose the one who had the bigger debt canceled."

Correctimundo! Jesus smiles at the woman and turns toward her, but he keeps watch on Simon. "You have judged correctly."

Interesting word choice on Jesus's part.

Simon bristles. But the woman! She is a *sinner* woman. She's a woman of ill repute. Everyone knows this of her. He glances at the faces of other men in the room. Some of them have probably employed her, um, services. How dare she blast past his servant and storm the house and practically accost his guest?

"Do you see this woman?" Jesus asks Simon.

Simon swallows like he's gulping down marbles. He nods.

"I came into your house. You did not give me any water for my feet, but she has wet my feet with her tears and wiped them with her hair. You did not give me a kiss, but this woman, from the time I entered, has not stopped kissing my feet. You did not put oil on my head, but she has poured perfume on my feet."

caught in the non-act

Simon bites the hook and starts to squirm. He knows. He has not fulfilled even the barest rule of hospitality, a rule as old as Father Abraham, from when he entertained the Lord and two angels at Mamre (see Genesis 18:1–8). You wash a guest's feet. You offer oil for his sun-parched skin. You kiss him in greeting. You welcome your guest with joy, regardless of the type of road he's traveled. And, oh yes, you feed him. But food is only part of the occasion. And today, all Simon has given Jesus is food. He has given him none of the treatment any guest deserves, let alone an honored teacher who holds people's attention like the wind holds a kite with its breath.

But he's always done everything right. He is the obedient one. He is a Pharisee, legal to the comma and quotation mark. He can recite all the laws, and he knows that Jesus is not supposed to be letting the likes of her touch him.

Simon hasn't figured this out yet, but Jesus knows: what we see is not who we are, and his deep work begins its way out from our hearts. In this woman, who has been forgiven the sins of her past, this "sinner woman," we see the miraculous. We see a woman given a new life, a new start, a true rebirth. We see that wondrous life overflow from her changed heart through her tears, drying his feet with her hair, and her loving administration of perfume.

This woman sinned with her body, and who of us hasn't sinned with our body? Making love when we didn't feel loving, or loving another physically in order to get our emotional needs met, or withholding physical love as a means of securing attention or showing reproach, or dressing in a way that draws inappropriate attention to us, or taking things to another level of sinning with our body, or overeating or under-eating, not exercising or over-doing the fitness routine, or hurting our body with too little sleep or medicating with substances?

Sin is sin, my friend, and Jesus knows this. Christ knows that Mr. Obedient Pharisee sins with his body and likely his thought life too, though in a different way than the woman pouring perfume over Jesus's feet.

reputation, repentance, relationship

Jesus watches Simon closely. "Therefore, I tell you, her many sins have been forgiven—for she loved much. But he who has been forgiven little loves little" (Luke 7:47).

Little sin. Little forgiveness. Little love. This splashes like an iron shoe into the little puddle of Simon's little-noticed soul. Why should he need forgiveness? He is obedient, after all. But deep down, he knows. Obedience without love equals hypocrisy. The letter of the law is cold and lifeless and loveless, just like Simon, and means nothing without the Spirit of the law alongside it, the Spirit who forgives, loves, offers and restores relationship.

Sometimes, "churchianity" feels like Simon. A room full of people who get it all right, everything except the loving. The self-righteous are so rarely full of love, so rarely spontaneous and forgiving. Instead they heap their coffers with the cold coins of their own do-gooding, wrapped in judgment of others whose sins are obvious, flagrant, like this woman with her "sinful" life. After all, it is one thing if you sin and keep quiet about it; then others don't know and you can keep up your image. But if you parade about in your sin, you are an embarrassment to the church and to God, so keep it quiet. Like the Pharisee.

The problems with this approach to living are enormous. Reputation is nothing without repentance, without the beauty of a forgiven and restored life. This is not to say that we should sin big so that we can experience a bigger love for God because he had such a big job to do to forgive us. But the consequence of sin, big or small, is the same: it separates us, rupturing our relationships with God, with others, and with ourselves.

What kind of relationship has Simon with God, with others, with himself? And though his sins may have seemed small, how small is it if you lose your heart? He has lost his heart all for the sake of appearing righteous, crossing all the Ts in the manuscript of his legalistic little life. But God wants so much more for us Simons of the world, so much more for us "sinner" women: God wants to rewrite the rules and give us a breathtaking bond with Jesus like this woman has, who burst into the room and burst into tears and burst into a radical relationship with Christ.

Yes, her sins were radical. Unforgivable, deserving stoning according to the letter of the Law. But if your heart, like Simon's, has turned to stone, then all the getting-it-right living amounts to nothing. And Christ offers each of us, Simon or sinner woman, the same gift: a radical new breath of life. Forgiveness.

face forward

Finally, Jesus turns to this woman, whose face shines beneath the veil of tears, whose entire countenance must be radiant from the outworking of Christ's love and mercy. He faces her, and says, "Your sins are forgiven."

He has heard her heart and read her very soul. As he looks into her eyes—*when did someone last meet your eyes, when did anyone ever love you with such a gaze, and by eye contact declare you valuable? Never, never!*—the affirmation alights in her heart like a dove: She is forgiven. She is loved. She is free.

I wish I could really see her face, really read the look in her eyes, the incredible release from all the sins of her past, the freedom from the wounds of her life and the rupturing sin against her as a woman, the abuse she has experienced by men who used her sexually and disregarded her soul. Yes, she was at the very least a loose woman, perhaps a prostitute; but one is not a prostitute if there are no customers, and men sinned when they came to her, then judged her for her sin.

And here is Jesus, the greatest teacher of all time, a man to whom crowds swarm for healing and wait in line, chase him for miles all over the countryside. Here is Jesus, meeting her eyes, loving her, forgiving her, and receiving the deepest gift she can give him—the gift of tears, hair, perfume, so much a picture of the essence of her femininity.

runway bright

I do see her face, every time I see my friend. Gorgeous of face and frame, she was sucked into the vortex of the fashion world, taunted with images of perfection. A full-blown eating disorder awaited her in the dark alleys behind the flashbulbs and fake sets. Layered beneath the disorder's costume was a longing for love, and promiscuity promised fulfillment for that longing. Her self-hatred knew no bounds until, in desperation, broken by binging and loathing, disabled by the judgmental world of cameras and agencies, she found Jesus.

You could light a theater from the glow on her face. The forgiveness she experiences from Christ, the take-your-breath-away relationship she has with him, the everydayness of his love for her…this is the picture of the woman with the flask of perfume, breaking it over Jesus, washing his feet with her tears.

What a fragrance, the broken-and-spilled-out gift of her past, poured out into an anointing oil of love, a gratitude deeper than any language in the world can convey.

Like the sinner woman, my friend's past became the gift she gave to Jesus—and the look he gives her now. "Be still my beating heart," as they say in those romance novels!

Hear his declaration again: "Your sins are forgiven."

Let those words soak into the neglected desert soil of your own soul. Your heart is parched for the love Jesus offers this woman, and you. Oh, to meet Jesus's eyes and receive that love.

You've tried so hard, and it's never good enough. Not good enough for your own high standards, or those of your husband or boyfriend or parents or boss. Or you quit trying because you knew you'd never measure up. You keep your secrets tucked away because no one will love you if they know the truth. You sit in the pew or on the padded chairs at church and look great, smile sweetly, sing earnestly, but inside, you know that you fail too often, sin too broadly.

Try this, then: List those sins that come to mind right away, the parts of your past that you have shielded from others, the little ugly shards of glass that you've buried in your backyard for so long. Your shame over your thought life, or your secret addictions, or your inability to love very well, or to receive love. Your distress over your relationships and your failures there. The mistakes you've made that even now you wish you could undo. The memories and regrets that never leave you, like killer bees in the attic of your mind, stinging you every time you venture near yet refusing to let you leave them alone. List those, all of them. Just write them down.

Now lift your eyes toward Jesus. Hear his words again: "Your sins, which are many, are forgiven" (see Luke 7:47). See Jesus turn his gaze toward you? He is meeting your eyes and eradicating all the shame you tote around in your pain-shriveled heart.

Your sins are forgiven.

Your sins are forgiven.

Your sins are forgiven.

Hear Jesus say this until you not only believe it but feel it, and then look in the mirror. The psalmist says, "They looked to Him and were radiant, and their faces shall never be ashamed" (34:5, NASB).

surprising forgiveness, overflowing gratitude

I love it that Jesus tells Simon that the woman's sins, which are many, are forgiven, and thus she loves so extravagantly. He wants to make sure that Simon gets it, that he understands exactly what he is saying, that the math adds up.

Some speculate that the wording is strange because the original language, Aramaic, lacked a word for "gratitude."[2] These folks say that if the words were actually translated correctly, the end of Jesus's question in Luke 7:42 would read, "Which will be more grateful?" Such an interesting question, since both of the people in Jesus's example were in debt, and had their debts forgiven. But the one who had the most mess forgiven would demonstrate—the tears, the hair, the perfume—the most gratitude. Would "love much."

In Simon's time, moneylenders were required to set people free from debt every seven years, but they devised all sorts of chicanery to avoid it, sliding people into prison, losing titles, whatever it took to keep the land and lock the legitimate owner away. The offer, then, of forgiveness of debt must surprise those gathered round Jesus, and set up within some a wistful longing, and in others the sting of conviction. And gratitude, something Simon never experiences (because, well, he's just nearly perfect the way he is, right?). Simon isn't in debt to anyone, because he's smarter than that.

So Jesus explains to Simon the woman's overflowing love.

Imagine Jesus looking Simon in the eyes, and how Simon must feel inside. How shrunken, a great nothingness, because he doesn't need forgiveness…or he doesn't think he needs it. But what a loss, because he doesn't get to experience this outpouring of gratitude for a gift undeserved. He doesn't get to meet Jesus's eyes with such abandon, such freedom, such start-over childlike trust.

Obviously Simon needs forgiveness, just as much as this fallen woman needs forgiveness, just as much as you and I need forgiveness. We can't live without it, and that's where we're so often left: not living, like Simon, who isn't really living, who's kept his hands clean, maybe, while his heart seethes with the snakes of self-righteousness.

In those days, like the debt issue, forgiveness wasn't offered as routine fare.[3] It wasn't something that people handed one another after an altercation, like a discount coupon good for the next round in the boxing ring. Priests could announce or pronounce forgiveness after a sin offering, but here is Jesus, forgiving, with no sacrifice to God in the temple! No wonder the room hisses with reaction. Jesus takes the place of the priests; he declares forgiveness and puts himself in the place of God. He offers what every single man and woman in the room so desperately want.

But wait: there has been a sacrifice. This woman sacrificed her pride, forsook her shame, and poured out her fragrant offering of gratitude on the public altar. She left the shadows of her sinful life, scraped together her courage, and brought the only gift she could to present to Jesus: the fragrant aroma of gratitude, from a heart fully forgiven.

peace at last

The guests erupt in whispers, covering their questions with their hands, "Who is this who even forgives sins?" (Luke 7:49). Some of them, undoubtedly, are angry, because Jesus is performing the function of the priests without the ceremony and off location. But others must react with wonder, and longing. "Who is this? He forgives sins?" Oh, to hear those words, to experience that themselves.

Others may wish that you would not walk in such blatant forgiveness, such showy gratitude, that your shame would continue to cling to you like plastic wrap on a humid day in July. Because your freedom convicts them of their enslavement, and sadly, it is more comfortable to wish you enslaved than for them to do the repentance that leads to forgiveness.

Don't listen to the eruptions from the crowd—let them whisper behind their hands. Go ahead, break open your flask and pour out your past; then listen to the great Teacher, the rule breaker, the radical.

Jesus says to the woman, to you, to me, "Your faith has saved you; go in peace." Then leave your perfume there, the fragrance of forgiveness lingering for days and weeks. Let Jesus meet your eyes, walk with you to the door, and into the rest of your life.

You are a new you, radiant with forgiveness, a woman whose past becomes the gift she offers the one who gives her new life.

come along to...

 · transfer from dark to light ·

Oh, God.
Here they are.
My list of secrets
My regrets and sins and sorrows
That I haul about and hang from my aching heart.
I lay it out before you.
Deepen my sorrow until my repentance overflows.
This is my perfume, this is my anointing oil,
This is the alabaster jar of my heart.
Free me from the debt
Of my years of regret.
Please forgive me,
And receive me
And the gift of my past.

• transfix upon Christ •

From that forgiving place, be still. Let the silence fill up with your gratitude and turn you to worship. In silence, without words, just love God in this time.

• translate the meaning •

- Who are the Simons in your life? When have you been the Simon, looking with judgment on others and forgetting to offer the bare minimum of hospitality to others, whether in your heart or in your home?
- In what ways do you identify with the "sinner woman"?
- What is the perfume in your flask, the oil of your past that you can pour out as a gift for Jesus? What sin have you carried about, its shame weighing you down? Make a list of your baggage, and give it to Jesus.
- What is the reading on your gratitude gauge? How do you show your love-reaction to Christ's forgiveness? When have you truly experienced forgiveness, really felt forgiven?
- In what ways do your past sin and your present forgiveness allow you to impact others' journeys?

• transform by renewing your mind •

I prayed to the LORD, and he answered me. He freed me from all my fears. Those who look to him for help will be radiant with joy; no shadow of shame will darken their faces. In my desperation I prayed, and the LORD listened; he saved me from all my troubles.

Psalm 34:4–6, NLT

• transparency through prayer •

Dear God,
My past weighs me down,
My secret regrets as heavy as stone.
I try to smile and look good,
But I know the truth.
I am not good enough.
And I have sinned, with my heart, my body, my
       mind.
I have separated myself from others and
ruptured my relationship with you.
And now, my breath comes in gasps.
I run to you, and past the judges at the door and
       around the table.
I run to you, and break open my past,
the vial of perfume from my illicit life.
It is all I have to give you.
It is my life, and I give it to you.
And you…you just look at me
Eyes brimming with love
And you receive my gift
And give me back my life.

Thank you.
Thank you.
Thank you.
Amen.

• transpired action •

How will you love radically today?

come along to the meadow

Illuminations on Growth

"Consider the lilies, how they grow."
—LUKE 12:27, NASB

Lead, kindly Light, amid the encircling gloom;
Lead thou me on!
The night is dark, and I am far from home;
Lead thou me on!
Keep thou my feet; I do not ask to see
The distant scene; one step enough for me.
—JOHN HENRY CARDINAL NEWMAN

At my folks' house, there is a doorjamb in the hallway with lines beginning lower than the doorknob. Each line is carefully notated with name and date. If you're a frequent visitor who appears to be short of topping off, you'll also get lined up against the doorjamb, heels carefully placed against the juncture of floor and wall, measured with a ruler perched on your head, parallel to the floor.

And the next time you visit, you will be measured again.

And I promise you will hear, "Look at how you've grown!" A grandparent may say, "Let's put a brick on your head so you'll slow down!" or, "The best favor he ever did his mother was waiting until he was born to grow like that." Adults will shake their heads, as though they have never seen anything like this in all their born days, as though you truly are a wonder, a one-of-a-kind genus…which you are.

So they will track your growth. "Look! You've grown three inches since last Thanksgiving." More wonderment in their eyes, and you will feel like you've been selected to be the first young astronaut in space, or you just won a blue ribbon and grand prize at the state fair.

What would it be like if we had a wall chart of our growth as individuals within a larger home, the church? What would it be like if I pressed my heels against the wall that is Jesus and stood up tall, head back, spine straight, bellybutton pressed to my back, to see how high I reach, compared to him? What if there were marks on the wall to measure how much I'd grown since my last visit?

When was that visit, anyway?

Last week, our son came busting through the door, excited about a new ministry team. "It's for people who are serious about growing, and serious about serving. It's been a long time since I grew spiritually." I look at him, a giant of a person in both height and heart, and marvel at this. He expects to grow, looks for growth, and when he doesn't see it, searches for it some more. A long time since he grew? He's only sixteen.

I marvel at this attitude, because I just want to get through the day. I want to be able to check off some stuff from my ever-growing list (and I'm so disappointed when something I've done isn't on the list!) and maybe find some of the wood underneath the piles on my desk and possibly put away the canned goods for the overflow pantry and, oh yes, collapse those boxes for recycling and—wow—a home-cooked dinner sure would be nice. Then I could go to bed before midnight so I can wake up and hit Snooze for an hour before rolling out of bed at 5:30 a.m. to do it again. On some days, when I look at the growth chart on the wall of my soul, I think it's been longer than he's been alive since I've grown.

Isn't it time we learned to act our age, isn't it time to grow into who we are created to be? If God allows us the years, or even if not, learn to grow up well, radiantly well.

Come along, then, to the meadow, and hear what Jesus has to say about growing up.

consider this

"Consider the lilies, how they grow," Jesus says (Luke 12:27, NASB). The people hang on his words like starving children in a bread line. He has been teaching them deep truths about prayer, and the real-life context of anxiety, and about forgiveness. Now he brings it home, makes it real. "Consider the lilies."

What's that about lilies? Jesus always has great object lessons, fabulous fodder for children's sermons at the synagogue. Hopefully the rabbis are taking notes. (They may be, but likely the notes concern an early draft of their diabolical plots.)

As I look out my window, the lilies are about the only thing along our fence line that grow by themselves. We didn't plant them, I certainly don't water them, and yet there they are: bright orange, ever bearing as long as someone, *ahem,* doesn't mow them down. The first time I picked a huge bouquet of daylilies, I was hosting a committee meeting in our ancient parsonage with its leaded glass windows and mirrors, the dark gleaming wood whispering secrets of the past. I carried the perky trumpet blooms with their extravagant foliage inside, filled a vase with our well water, and placed the flowers on a side table. They smiled like tiny balloons in the children's ward at the hospital, happy to give grace whether anyone noticed or not.

By the time the committee members arrived, however, those lilies tattled a different story. Smooshed and wilted, the blooms lay strewn about the table, more reminiscent of a battlefield than a sweet meeting of blue-haired ladies, myself, and a toddler or two. When I moaned about the fallen, a bit embarrassed because I thought I'd done something wrong, one of the dear women said, "Maybe that's why they're called daylilies. They only last one day. But more will open tomorrow." I still can see her gentle smile.

More did open the next day, and the next, and the next, until the blooms were miniature and faded as though they'd been washed too many times with bleach. But they continued to bud, even inside my home. Lilies just grow. They grow without particular help from gardeners; at least, these lilies do. They grow, and it is expected—they are geared for growth, and so they grow. They grow until winter, and then rest, and then they grow again, persistent in their greenery and their colorful blossoms.

Somehow, I lost the application for my own life. I consider the lilies, like Jesus says, but I always look at it as, "God will take care of all my needs." And this is true. He has seen to my needs in millions of visible ways and trillions of unnoticed ways, and definitely this is a key application of Jesus's example. But also tucked into the corner of this picture is another dimension. He means that we will, like the lilies, continue to grow. That we will grow, and grow, and grow in all ways, until one day, we are in full bloom.

I'm afraid, when I look at my own life, I've forgotten this principle, this assumption that I will continue to grow until the day Jesus calls for me and takes me to heaven. *Full bloom* for me means something like bloating, or the idea of reaching middle age and being termed a "full-bloom" lady, which I guess is a shade better than saying, "Honey, the bloom is off the rose." Or my only measurement for growth is girth, which means my waistbands won't fit, so no-growth fits the standard just fine. But growth is far more than girth, or the aging of our bodies.

The Scriptures tell us of John the Baptist, who "grew and became strong in spirit; and he lived in the desert until he appeared publicly to Israel" (Luke 1:80). And of Jesus himself: "And the child grew and became strong; he was filled with wisdom, and the grace of God was upon him" (2:40). And again, "And Jesus grew in wisdom and stature, and in favor with God and men" (verse 52).

Paul states it flatly for us: "Stop thinking like children. In regard to evil be infants, but in your thinking be adults" (1 Corinthians 14:20).

It really is time, as Jesus said, to consider the lilies, and how they grow. If God is so concerned with the birth-to-full-bloom life cycle of the lily, how much more concerned is God with our growing up? We expect our kids to grow up, and our grass and our trees to mature, and if any of these three don't grow we call in experts to help. We hope our husband or boyfriend will grow… and surely we expect ourselves to grow, as well.

growth expectation

Considering those lilies, it seems that growth is natural unless you're dead, or unless it's autumn when plants are tucking themselves into bed for extended naps, or it's winter while they're snuggled into their long sleep. The expectation of growth permeates the Scriptures as well.

We're meant to "grow in the grace and knowledge of our Lord and Savior Jesus Christ" (2 Peter 3:18). This one gives me pause. I have a coffee cup with my name and its meaning on it: Jane— God Is Gracious. The name *Jane* also means "God's gracious gift," but I can attest to the fact that I'm not always God's gracious gift to my loved ones. For the longest time I was too ashamed to use the mug for my morning slug of coffee because I was so definitely not gracious, not a gift. I was grumpy and anxious and just plain mean too often.

This natural bent toward sin and ugliness doesn't alleviate me of the desperate need to experience grace, and to grow in the grace of our Lord Jesus. Grace, it turns out, is not something you *do*. It is a gift, divine mercy or favor or assistance that we cannot earn and don't deserve in the least. It is something that we learn to live in the midst of, relinquishing our own inabilities and disabilities and relaxing into that gift that is heavenly help. Grace, as Gerald May said, threatens all my normalities.[1]

So growing in the grace of the Lord Jesus looks like increasingly knowing and experiencing his love, and in turn offering that love to others, undeserving though they are. Growth in grace, in my case, is not a natural process. It's a supernatural and lifelong exchange of God's love for my scrawny ability to love, a love that I then share, even if like a very bad, low-resolution fax transmission, with others.

and that's not all

In addition to grace, we're to grow in the knowledge of the Lord Jesus and in the knowledge of God (2 Peter 3:18 and Colossians 1:10). This doesn't mean, "Take some seminary courses and memorize some books of the Bible and get your doctrine all straightened out so your head is crammed with a bunch of facts." Certainly those are good, but growing in grace starts out meaning to know him—know Jesus and know God, just as you would get to know an acquaintance, who then becomes a friend, who then becomes a lifelong companion. This growth-in-grace idea carries the element of the discovery of relationship and the deepening of understanding, an endless uncovering of who God is and who Jesus is.

An old adage declares that in a good marriage, you keep discovering new things about your spouse. While I think Rich learned anything even remotely interesting that there was to know about me before we even got engaged, I continue to hear parts of his life that I'd never known before: a job he had, a ministry he served in prior to seminary, a crazy story from his cross-country team. Even more than that, I learn about a gift that hadn't shown up before or a longing he'd buried all his life that was being fulfilled, and seeing these new things in him deepens my love for him.

So it is with God. The more we know God, the more deeply we love God. Part of that mystery of relationship, of knowing God, is revealed as we heed 1 Peter 2:2 (NASB), "like newborn babes, long for the pure milk of the word, that by it you may grow in respect to salvation."

Longing for the pure milk of the Word. I understand what it means to long when I remember my decision as a first-time mom to wean our baby. I didn't ask anyone how to do this. I simply stopped breast-feeding her. I've never known such pain, both physical and emotional, and neither had she—she cried for me, reached her little arms to me, and squiggled in her daddy's hug while he tried to feed her from a bottle. She leaned away from him and hung over the side of his forearm, desperate for the real milk and the comfort that comes from such nurturing closeness.

Imagine what it would be like if we so craved the pure milk of the Word that we wriggled out of competing obligations and ran toward God through Scripture. Consider what would happen "that by it you may grow in respect to salvation." The word *salvation* here doesn't mean "initial conversion"—its root is *salve,* "an ointment used for healing." *Salvation* here means "growing into full maturity."[2]

Consider the lilies! Crave the Word so you can bloom.

"Now that you have tasted of the kindness of the Lord." In the original language, the word for "kindness" could have meant "delicious."[3] What a yummy thought! The deliciousness of God! I love this image, so different from our stern father picture of never getting it right, of judgment and more judgment; such a picture of Scripture as a feast, not a duty, as a joy. As Jeremiah said, "Thy words were found and I ate them, and Thy words became for me a joy and the delight of my heart; for I have been called by Thy name, O LORD God of hosts" (Jeremiah 15:16, NASB). Why are they a joy? Because we have been called by Jesus's name, into his family, and he speaks to us now, today, through those very words. What a delicious delight, indeed. What a way to grow.

Jewish friends tell me that when their children are in Hebrew school, the rabbi instructs them to open their Scriptures to Psalm 119, the stunning passage about the delights of God's Word. The children place a square of wax paper over verse 103, "How sweet are your words to my taste, sweeter than honey to my mouth!" The rabbi plops a dollop of honey right over that verse. They taste, they see that the Lord is good, that his word is sweet. Oh, that we might taste and know God's sweetness, God's deliciousness, through his Word. We would never need chocolate again... or, at least, not for the same reasons.

So try this, when it comes to craving the milk of the Word: when you have a day off from work, or are on a personal retreat, try a fast from all other words except Scripture. Don't read the newspaper, the ingredients on the rice mix at the grocery store, the tabloid headlines, the back of the cereal box, or the papers in your child's backpack. Fix your eyes only on Scripture, and see how sweet becomes God's pure Word.

lines on the doorjamb

But these are not the only marks on the walls of our souls. As we consider the lilies, as we settle into the growth cycle of our lives, Paul says, "Your faith is growing more and more, and the love every one of you has for each other is increasing" (2 Thessalonians 1:3). These are not the standards society sets for us (your income better grow, your house should grow, your waist will probably grow, your investments must grow) and maybe not the growth marks for our church either. Growth in churches is often measured more in numbers than in size of faith, than in the amount of loving going on. How many new members? How many "saved"? What about the budget? How much salary is the pastor making (and why)? How many parking spaces are there, and do we need more?

No, Paul is just repeating Jesus's yardstick: "Love the Lord your God with all your heart, and with all your soul, and with all your mind, and with all your strength" and "your neighbor as yourself" (Mark 12:30–31, NASB). What a church the believers of Thessalonica convened. They loved each other "abundantly" in some renderings, to such an extent that the Word spread like brush fire in a drought. They developed a reputation for loving. Their love became a measure for others' effectiveness in growth, not whether that growth resulted in a megachurch or a monster budget or even a well-stocked supply closet or hundreds of small groups that meet each week. Rather, the measuring stick regards love and growing in love—love that's deeper, reaches further, and lasts longer.

How do we grow in love? Like a muscle, love develops as we exercise it, as we love others—like the Grinch who stole Christmas, whose heart "grew three sizes that day."

It helps to share our faith journeys with one another, to walk alongside each other on the same road. Second Thessalonians 1:4 recounts the church's "perseverance and faith in all the persecutions and trials" that they experienced. For us, too, walking through the fire together creates lifelong companions.

As we stand fast, believing by faith that God is bigger than our eyes can see, that God has plans beyond the difficulties of our lives, that God's intent toward us is good though life is hard—as we fix our eyes not on what is seen but on what is unseen, then our faith expands. We can know, absolutely know, in the company of our family of faith, that every single hardship either counts for eternity because it creates growth in us, or it counts for nothing. This is like standing together and bailing out water of the oft-sinking boat that is our lives—as we struggle together and help one another, we grow in faith and in grace and in love for one another. The result is like ripples of the water around that boat: others will see that love, see Jesus, and when we love them in practical ways, our faith grows and our love grows yet some more.

Grab a marker and make a line on the doorjamb, would you, please?

optimum soil

Good compost makes for good soil and creates an ideal condition for growing. Wilted, dying, cast-off vegetation, old roots, limbs, broken branches, grass clippings, and manure all contribute to compost, or decomposing organic matter.

"Consider the lilies," Jesus says, and all this considering is in the context of serious growth-enhancing compost. In Matthew 6, he couches the command in the midst of rich possibility, places where we easily could choose death instead of growth, failure to thrive instead of blooming. If everything we encounter, every situation, offers the possibility of growth, then it also offers the possibility of refusing growth. So Jesus lists serious hindrances to our salvation, to our growing to full maturity: money, worry, judging others; and in Luke 12, Jesus covers other decomposing ingredients, such as hypocrisy and envy.

Who doesn't worry about money? I don't know a single person who is worry free about their finances, who doesn't occasionally or frequently obsess about whether they'll be okay, be able to pay the bills, keep the house, put the kids through school, and retire without living in poverty. For many who live one month away from eviction from their nice homes, the issue of money will halt their growth.

Money gives us something to worry about, and worry we do. We wring our hands and pitch our problems to God, then grab them back. We are like washerwomen, hands red from lye soap and washing and wringing and wringing some more.

"Consider the lilies," Jesus said, "how they neither toil nor spin." But I toil. I spin. I'm a veritable whirling dervish, a ride at the amusement park that isn't the least amusing.

Judging, hypocrisy, envy—what a growth-evading detour these little habits offer. Each state seems to say, "Avoid growing, just indulge." Each state is other-focused, a sure way to avoid maturity. Fixate on others' lives, their sins, their habits, the ways they hurt or shame you, or have it in for you. Blame others for your problems, if possible. Worry about what others have and what you don't: the car or spouse or child or job or landscaping or past or future. Let envy squirm around in your soul. Then see how much you grow...or *don't* grow, because that worm will nibble your plant down to nothing.

The compost, you see, is composed of the scraps, leftovers, and refuse of our lives. When we gather these uglies of worry and money and judging and envy together and pile them up, and don't allow them to sit inside our souls, they become a nutrient-rich fertilizer, an organic root stimulator. Then, like the lilies, we will grow.

soul-grow

We've had more rain this August than in one hundred years. And with the rains comes green grass, Emerald City green. And mosquitoes the size of those flying monkeys too—they will carry you away unless you wear sandbags on your ankles. Maybe you've had too many rains in your life, thank you very much. More than enough mosquitoes, attacking from every direction; so much compost that unless it's mixed with some plain old dirt, it will scorch the roots of your soul.

But the one who said, "Consider the lilies, how they grow," is also our Master Gardener. Let him determine where you are on the growth chart. Let Jesus tend to your sensitive roots and your tenuous blooms. Just relax into his care. You are of far more worth than the lilies, and they neither toil nor spin. So don't toil. Don't spin. Just do what plants do, what children do: grow.

And then, at the right time, press your heels against the wall that is Jesus, and hear him say, "My, how you've grown." Bask in his radiant smile. You may see him shake his head in total wonder, as though he's never seen anyone like you before.

Because that's the truth.

come along to...

 • transfer from dark to light •

Dear God,
I've neglected the lilies.
I've forgotten about growing,
I've fixated on the composts
Of money, and worry, and
My neighbors' stuff
And avoided pressing
Against the doorjamb
To see how I have grown.

I confess that this has been a
Failure-to-thrive season,
And I repent of this.
I have concocted all kinds of reasons
To not grow
And this is sin.

Growth is my choice and
My responsibility.
Forgive me, please,
For not growing.
And grant me the grace
To press into your love
And grow.

• transfix upon Christ •

"Consider the lilies," and just be still. Their language is beauty, and stillness. Don't try to use words; just wait, glowing with the beauty that comes from being deeply loved. Be still, and let God love you just as you are. Set aside your own standards and high expectations, or lack of expectations, and just be still.

• translate the meaning •

- We often think about being better at our roles. But if we want to grow in our roles, we have to grow in our souls. Where do you need to grow emotionally, spiritually, intellectually? What is a grow-up task concerning your physical self-care?
- Aging may be inevitable; maturity is optional, regardless of your chronological age. When do you excuse yourself from growing? What would others say if you asked them, "Where do you see growth in my life? Where do you think I need to mature?"

- Where is the expectation that you will grow up? When do you bow out of growth with "I can't help it—that's just the way I am" excuses? Where does that reaction come from?

- Evaluate the areas of growing up: in grace, in relationship with God and Jesus Christ, in faith, in love for one another. In what ways can you seek growth in these areas?

- Consider the lilies, and the compost. What are your ideal conditions for blooming? How do worry, money, envy, judging divert your attention from growth? How can they convert and become compost, helping you grow?

• transform by renewing your mind •

For this reason, since the day we heard about you, we have not stopped praying for you and asking God to fill you with the knowledge of his will through all spiritual wisdom and understanding. And we pray this in order that you may live a life worthy of the Lord and may please him in every way: bearing fruit in every good work, growing in the knowledge of God, being strengthened with all power according to his glorious might so that you may have great endurance and patience, and joyfully giving thanks to the Father, who has qualified you to share in the inheritance of the saints in the kingdom of light.

Colossians 1:9–12

• transparency through prayer •

Dear God,
I want to consider the lilies.
I want to grow.
I want to grow up
Into the person you've dreamt me to be.
And so
If you'll lend me your hand
I'll stand up straight
In full forgiveness
And do what children do.
Grow.
Thank you.
In Jesus,
Amen.

• transpired action •

How is God calling you to "grow up" today?

come along
to the synagogue

Illuminations on Hope

"Should not this woman…be set
free on the Sabbath day?"
—LUKE 13:16

If you do not hope, you will not find
out what is beyond your hopes.
—CLEMENT OF ALEXANDRIA

Throwing the car into park, I mark down my mileage and push open the heavy car door. Load up everything I can carry in one trip and head for the house. But the door is locked, and I kick it in frustration, dropping my belongings and raging (quietly, of course, lest the neighbors notice) while I dig for my keys. And then the key doesn't work because it requires both hands and a tricky little routine of stomp-pull-kick-push to get the sticky, thick, dumb door open, all the while turning the key, and so I drop the rest of my burdens and kick the door out of sequence because of my anger.

Heaven forbid that I ring the doorbell and rouse someone from the nether regions of the household to come and open the door and help me with my carrying, something they would gladly do. I think they should intuit that I am home. They should hear the loud muffler or be watching for the sweep of headlights as I pull into the driveway. They should have the door unlocked and stand at attention, ready to haul.

I keep silent. My list of tasks and expectations grows, and so I set my alarm a little earlier, increase my expectations of myself, load up myself with weights impossible to carry alone. I've always lived this way. One of my character defects contains the little tiny rule, "Competent women must do it all."

So my list grows, along with the circles under my eyes; when I can't meet my own expectations, my family lovingly picks up the dropped parcels and mops up the spilled expectations.

This makes me crazy, because I have this rule of taking care of things myself, and though I know they pick up and mop up out of love, I interpret this wrongly: I see that I've failed, that I'm incompetent. I see their help as judgment.

And so I work harder, try to sleep less, try to get it all done by myself.

This does not do wonders for family life, because their gift to me is a gift of kindness, of grace, of reprieve, and when I work harder, and snap because their standards are not as high as mine, the wounded pile up around me. Then shame leers its gargoyle face, telling me that other women get it all done. They don't even have cobwebs in the corners of their living rooms and windowsills, and my living room looks like I decorated for Halloween…except it's June.

Where do we get the idea that we must do everything by ourselves, no rest for the weary and all that jazz? With that rule, we're about as radiant as a wet matchstick, and we work hard at everything…except, perhaps, hope.

Jesus invites us to come alongside him, sit in on a session at the synagogue, and meet a woman who knew she couldn't do it all. Come along, meet a woman who never gave up hope.

at right angles for healing

Her body locked into a right angle eighteen years ago, and since then she's seen nothing but the ground when she stands on her feet. If she sits, the world resumes proper perspective, but she can only sit for so long before the sores develop. So she trundles along with the ungainly gait of a praying mantis whose wings have iced up. Years ago her neck froze into place, as though the vertebrae glued themselves together, so that even turning her head creates razors of pain. She can only raise her head an inch or so, enough to see a couple of steps farther (see Luke 13:10–17).

The muscles in the backs of her legs contract painfully in any other position. But she faithfully goes to the synagogue, hears the reading of the Scriptures, and listens to the teaching that follows. Every Sabbath she hopes; every seventh day when the Jewish world rests from its labors, her heart works hard to hope. For fifty-two

Sabbaths a year, for eighteen years, hope is hard work, hard to sustain, hard to believe in a God who never answers.

But she doesn't quit. She never gives up. Even though the sympathy of her family and friends dried up in a drought of disbelief and disappointment long ago, she still hopes, even though the accusations still rankle: "If you had more faith, you would be healed." "You must have really done something wrong for God to punish you like this." "You have a demon!"

She cannot afford to lose hope, because without hope, she knows she will die. She clings to hope like a cliff climber clings to the rockface, knowing hope to be irrational, knowing that hope, though invisible, is stronger than her beating heart. Hope is the drumbeat of her very soul, setting the rhythm of her days, forcing her footsteps to keep moving ahead.

This day, this Sabbath, she plunges forward to the synagogue, barely noticing the familiar landmarks at the edges of her peripheral vision. She has memorized the path, the stones, the dust. This day of rest, her heart keeps working hard, beating with every step: *Hope. Hope. Hope.* Even though she's spent so much of her life doubled over, she remembers the sky, the joy of walking with her head held high. She remembers. And so she hopes.

a calling

Her breath quickens as she draws near. Hope pounds, that futile but never-ending thud that starts from far outside her realm of reason: relentless hope, the rhythm of heaven. She hurries in her headlong position and stands, face toward the floor, legs and neck and back aching, heart slamming against her sternum from her journey.

His voice, as he reads from the Torah, steals her breath. She cannot see him, but the timbre of his words rolls over her like a soft wave from a gentle summer sea. Even in her awkward position, she relaxes into the combination of God's Word and the rich voice…and something else. Something within responds; the hope activates itself like yeast mixed with warm water and honey.

And then she hears, "Woman, come forward!" Much bustling occurs but she doesn't understand. People scuttle out of the way. The Teacher has called her! A woman, a cripple, surely afflicted with a demonic presence, surely an unclean woman, relegated to the hopeless, hapless pile of unanswered, unexplained prayer problems.

He calls *her*.

When she reaches the front, the hope-beat within nearly deafens her. Even so, she is unprepared. He puts his hands on her—how long since someone touched her? Too long—and then his words ring with authority.

"Woman, you are set free from your infirmity."

The hinges in her body unlock, and without will of her own, her body springs up. Immediately her tongue loosens as well, and she praises God. Exultation tumbles from her lips, her hands rise toward heaven, and glory fills the room. Miraculous wonder shakes the people who watch, shakes her.

uproar

This shakes the establishment as well, but it shows up as rage, not wonder. The synagogue rulers surge forward, lava spewing from a trembling volcano. The rulers shout at the assembly, warning them, reminding them of the rules: "There are six days for work. So come and be healed on those days, not on the Sabbath."

She can hardly believe it. She almost laughs. Is there a day more appropriate for healing than the Sabbath? But people have always tried to keep God contained in a small box, like a keepsake locket, forcing God into an understandable and limited circumference. She saw this from her tiny window on the world for the past eighteen years. As she watched the narrow path beneath her feet, her faith expanded. Her binding created the soil for a hope that would not die. Too bad that as the Pharisees' rules for God grew, their faith diminished and their love disappeared like soap bubbles exploding against jagged stone.

The praise on her lips refuses to be bound, and mirth sparkles from her. The woman cannot drag her gaze from the Teacher, nor the smile from her mouth. It pushes clear into her cheekbones. She feels her face might split from joy.

The Teacher thunders his response. "You hypocrites! Doesn't each of you on the Sabbath untie his ox or donkey from the stall and lead it out to give it water? Then should not this woman, a daughter of Abraham, whom Satan has kept bound for eighteen long years, be set free on the Sabbath day from what bound her?"

All around the room, the people cheer, delighted with the Teacher, the wondrous display of God from him—all, that is, except for the Pharisees, the leaders in the synagogue.

their own bondage

The Pharisees hated Jesus for coming into their complacent, top-dog position—for healing people on the Sabbath, the day of rest.

No wonder the Pharisees couldn't cheer. They had no notes in their songs if the theme was healing, life, hope. Their hopes were firmly planted on their own ability to keep the Law, to adhere to the traditions that continued to expand like mold spores in humidity. They had created their own bondages through their rules for living. Jesus called them hypocrites because they spoke of rest, and yet their faith involved only rule upon rule. Surely they were right that the Sabbath was for rest, not working—God did say that, after all—but *they* defined how that would look. The tapestry of their definition became more and more elaborate, layers and layers of threads, until the thickness of their rules defied reality and entirely ruled out soul rest.

Though the Pharisees didn't believe in work on the Sabbath, their consciences were rest-less with their work motif and the disgrace they heaped on others. And so, here they watched like vultures from their seats in the synagogue, leaping on anyone who dared step outside their definitions of proper Sabbath keeping.

We are the same. We create our Sunday-in-a-box, our picture of what is appropriate for our worship service, what kind of music, liturgy, prayers; what sort of expectations, what we will expect from others, from God. We have our letter of the law, after all, and we do it to ourselves, as well. We *should* be able to do it all.

How do we incorporate hope into our days, our weeks, our lives? How about spreading out faith throughout your waking moments, creating pockets of time when you focus solely on hope? On what is your hope based, or on whom? Where do you feel hope, right now, this minute? And is it even possible that into that hope might come healing?

No. Absolutely not. As far as the Pharisees are concerned, hope shouldn't look like or lead to healing—healing is for the other six days. Far be it from God to choose to heal on the Sabbath, to give life on the Sabbath, restore what the Enemy has plundered and imprisoned for eighteen minutes or eighteen days or eighteen months or eighteen years. No, not healing, not on the Sabbath.

And that is the question we are left with: what would be healing for you today, tomorrow, any day, especially Sunday? Regardless of the day of the week or how many minutes in that day you allocate, what would give life? What will it take for you to give up the "I'll do it all, do it myself" approach to life and faith?

Trusting God to work while we heal requires faith, and faith requires hope, but God cannot be anything but faithful.

faith defies gravity

If that's a question for you—God's faithfulness—look again at the account. A woman in this culture was considered to be about as esteemed as a domestic dog. Even the Pharisees clearly prized an ox or a donkey enough to feed it and water it and exercise it.

Then here is Jesus doing more than leading this woman to food and water. He leads her to freedom, life, and healing. He calls the Pharisees on their inconsistent and degrading value system; one simply needn't bother to argue with Jesus. He is the ultimate lawyer, blending reason and reality into an immutable, irrefutable truth, as solid as a mountain of marble.

No wonder the Pharisees, rendered mute and stupid by Jesus's response, blush and clamp their mouths shut tight. But their fury mounts, and it won't be long before their humiliation leads them to treachery.

This is always a temptation for us, when proven wrong, when our words resound with brashness, when we lob our biases into the air like gold dust that instead turns out to be sawdust, much to our shame. We want to be right. We want God to act like we think he should act. We want to control the uncontrollable God of the universe by determining when he will heal. We want to be in charge and do it alone and do it our way.

And sometimes (I say this with fear and trembling), we decide that because God does not act as we think he should act, that perhaps the Scriptures are not true, that all we know or are taught about God is false because there's this portion of God that we don't understand. So we pick and choose, or cut out entirely, part of our faith that actually requires, well…faith.

Make no mistake. God will heal if and when he chooses, and all our timetables, all our rules, matter not to him. And so our job, daily, is to do as this woman does: hope. She keeps coming to God. She doesn't sit stewing at home in the dark, bent double by her own personal demon. Out she hobbles, with her eyes cast downward but a heart that refuses to be cast down. Her heart defies gravity. She seeks out God, attends synagogue, listens to God's Word. And she does not give up. She holds tightly to the balloon string of hope, knowing that one day God will fill that balloon and raise her up. One day, one way or another.

We cannot excise the faith part of our faith journey. Without faith, we have no journey at all. Without faith, we have no hope. Without faith in God—God who is inscrutable but good, indefinable but holy, unsearchable but just—we have no life. No, we must decide about God based on what we know to be true about God, not on what we do not know or do not understand. We must let God define healing.

the work of healing

Day of rest or not, healing sometimes is work. Sometimes the hinges do not loosen automatically, like oil on the rust-eaten Tin Man in *The Wizard of Oz*. Sometimes, the hinges of our souls are bound by years of neglect from others or self, or emotional abuse, or wounded memories. These wounds and bindings may call for deliberate work to heal.

One friend, who for years struggled with her drinking, still goes to a support group several times a week, still has a sponsor in whom to confide, who asks her hard questions and calls her to account for her emotional and physical well-being. She continues to do the work of healing, seven days a week, knowing that sobriety is worth every ounce of effort and energy required.

Another friend, whose father never affirmed her, who told her in word and action throughout her entire life that she was not valuable if she was not perfect, wrestles with how she hears others' words, how she interprets incidents in her life, how she views God. Because she cannot see the truth by herself, she's engaged a woman who specializes in care of the soul, who regularly asks her, "What is God trying to tell you in this situation? What are you reading into this that is not true, is not there?"

As in physical rehabilitation after an accident, retraining our muscles to do what they once did naturally, the soul also requires hands-on work to ensure the completion of healing. We may have no idea what "normal" looks like when it comes to healing. Like the blind person who suddenly regains sight and must learn to integrate what he knows from feeling and hearing with what his eyes suddenly perceive, the soul must learn to "read" with the heart what once was only understood through the mind, knowledge, or past experience.

So we can surround ourselves with people who will help us integrate what we know about God with what we need to learn about healing: wise mentors, people farther along the path than we are, who have endured their share of bent-double days and know exactly what we experience. Such people can challenge us to work the atrophied muscles of the soul and mind and heart, to develop the sustaining muscle called hope. And from that hope and healing flows praise, and from praise, deeper healing, even greater hope.

freedom of praise

One important characteristic stands out about this woman who is set free from her bondage. She doesn't get caught up in resentment or anger—these are her people! Her church! Why are they angry that she is healed on the Sabbath? Why aren't they rejoicing with her? Why don't they understand she is worth more than their oxen or donkeys? No, she doesn't let their pettiness and law banging diminish her joy. She will allow nothing and no one to rob her of that long-awaited blessing. I love her automatic, immediate expression of healing: she rises up and praises God.

Surely praise must have been her habit all along. That while her visual and physical world narrowed, her soul expanded through praise. Otherwise, how could this be her instant reaction, her gut reply to such a miracle? And when we lift our hands and holler, "Hallelujah!" the whole earth stands at attention and sucks in its breath, because praise is due the Creator of the universe and the Author of our healing.

A friend who studies Hebrew tells me that Orthodox Jews are to praise God one hundred times a day! Praise is a choice, a discipline, and it creates room for God to act, as Henri Nouwen defined discipline. What we know to be true about praise is that at the name of Jesus, the devil runs, and when we praise God, demons flee.

Sometimes, when I'm up to no good as far as the Enemy is concerned, he deviously tries to attack me with vertigo. It may be so severe that if I even move my finger while lying on the bed, the room will spin and whirl and my whole body will react.

The last time this happened, I was in the middle of serious writing with a crushing schedule. I lay down on the bed and looked outside, and the world shifted, the trees moved over, as though a plate had slammed inside my head and pushed me into a different frame of the viewfinder. I rolled to my back, eyes open to the ceiling, and groaned.

Then I heard, very clearly, *Praise. Raise your hands, and praise me.*

Immediately I knew that the kingdom of God was at hand. I raised my hands and praised: every person, every thing, every act I could think of; I praised God for creating and providing. For many minutes this went on, and I sensed that behind the curtain of the visible, beneath my praise, warfare occurred.

My vertigo fled after thirty minutes. I was so grateful. I lay on the bed for another spell of time, just rejoicing in the power of the name of Jesus. And I understood anew: no wonder the woman could stand upright.

woman, daughter of Abraham

Oh, what music it must be to the afflicted to hear Jesus call so affectionately—especially to the woman in Luke 13, to hear Jesus call her, "Woman," and confirm her identity, her belonging in the family tree of Abraham, to take her place once again with her people and stand aright with her hands uplifted and heart buoyant with Jesus's love. His very call, his words and direct seeing of her, healed her as well as his touch.

How to let Jesus touch us in this way?

What if you were to try listing those wounds that bend you in half, that fold your hope down the middle and cut you in two? List them in red ink, bleeding onto the paper. Then wait with your list and repeat those words from Jesus: "Woman, you are set free from your infirmity. You, daughter of Abraham, my child, you are set free in your spirit to be the woman I created you to be. Rise up!"

Whose voice will you let define you? The forked-tongue voice of the Pharisees? Or the voice of Jesus? Will you go it alone, or go forward when Jesus calls you and let him help you? Will you rise up with the radiance that comes from praise? Will you be bent double by the rules you've been taught and have embraced for your entire life, or will you let the Spirit set you free, that you might be free indeed?

Let's go with the voice of Jesus, with the Spirit who sets us free.

"Woman, you are set free from your infirmity."

come along to...

 • transfer from dark to light •

Dear God,
I have given away so much
Because I chose to focus on the ground
And be bent double at the waist
By the wounds of life.
But now, I know the truth.
I want to be set free from my
Infirmity,
I want to stand upright with
My hands raised in praise.
I give you the aching, breaking of my heart
The folding
Spindling
Mutilating of my soul.
And I ask that you restore me,
That you forgive me and raise me up.

• transfix upon Christ •

Hear Jesus's words again: "Woman, you are set free from your infirmity." List your "infirmities" and then just sit still. Wait. Don't speak, don't feel like you need to convince God to fix your problems, heal your pain, straighten out your bent-over back. Just be still, and breathe in God's presence, and let this resting silence bring its own healing.

• translate the meaning •

- What is your version of "do everything without help"?
- How can you incorporate hope into your day? Where do you find hope, and when? What interferes with hope for you? And what would healing look like for you, on a daily basis? Regardless of the day of the week or how many minutes in that day you allocate, what would give life? If you were to take a mini-rest each day, how would that look? Every single day has room for healing, for trusting God to be faithful.
- Where have you experienced healing? Where have you felt the judgment of the Pharisees? Remember that some people simply cannot rejoice in the work God does in someone else, because God has not chosen to act that way in their own lives.
- Make your red-ink list of the wounds that fold your soul in half, that bend your spirit double and bind you. Now,

take that list and deliberately place it on the floor, like a faith offering, and invite Jesus into the process of healing. Let him define what healing will look like, and ask him how you can participate in that process. You might even try standing up and bending over at the waist, like the woman in Luke 13:10–17. Stay in that position, aware of the list you've just created, and then, one by one, relinquish the items to God. Straighten up, slowly, and feel the weight disappear.

- Consider praise as a discipline. What if you set aside just three minutes today to praise God? What would you expect? What worries you about that? How can you make that happen?

• transform by renewing your mind •

I will praise you, O LORD, with all my heart; I will tell of all your wonders. I will be glad and rejoice in you; I will sing praise to your name, O Most High.… The LORD is a refuge for the oppressed, a stronghold in times of trouble. Those who know your name will trust in you, for you, LORD, have never forsaken those who seek you. Sing praises to the LORD, enthroned in Zion; proclaim among the nations what he has done.

Psalm 9:1–2, 9–11

Therefore, since we have been justified through faith, we have peace with God through our Lord Jesus Christ, through whom we have gained access by faith into this grace in which we now stand. And we rejoice in the hope of the glory of God. Not only so, but we also rejoice in our sufferings, because we know that suffering produces perseverance; perseverance, character; and character, hope. And hope does not disappoint us, because God has poured out his love into our hearts by the Holy Spirit, whom he has given us.

Romans 5:1–5

• transparency through prayer •

Oh, God,
How I rejoice that you are the God who heals,
You are the one in whom is all my hope.
No longer will I let my infirmities cripple me,
No longer will I bend beneath the weight of loss,
Sorrow, judgment.
Thank you, thank you for
Removing the law of gravity
And replacing it with the helium of Love,
For raising my heart like a balloon into the air
And my praise like a song born on the wind.
You are worthy of praise,
And I rejoice that you are the God who heals.
I choose, this day, to live in that healing,
To focus on your eyes
To revel in your love

To stand upright among those who don't believe.
May praise always tumble from my lips.
For you are the God who heals, the God of hope.
In Jesus's mighty name,
Amen.

• transpired action •

How will you find hope today?

come along to the plains

Illuminations on a Clean Heart

"What goes into a man's mouth does
not make him 'unclean,' but what
comes out of his mouth, that
is what makes him 'unclean.'"
—MATTHEW 15:11

The Christian thinks any good he does
comes from the Christ-life inside him.
He does not think God will love us
because we are good, but that God will
make us good because He loves us; just as
the roof of a greenhouse does not attract
the sun because it is bright, but becomes
bright because the sun shines on it.
—C. S. LEWIS

The young man glanced in the rearview mirror at the swirling red and blue lights. His heart slid down into his stomach, bubbling with anxiety.

The officer strode to the window. "License, please."

He handed over the license with shaking fingers.

"Why are you so nervous?" The officer's eyebrows rose like antennae. He didn't wait for an answer. "Okay, out of the car. I'm going to search your vehicle."

Though he didn't have a search warrant, and had no apparent reason to search the car other than the driver's anxiety, search it he did over the driver's protests. "You do not have my permission to search the car," he said, over and over.

It was an illegal search, and the warning for a loose brake light turned into an arrest for possession. Because the driver of the car was "driving dirty," as they say. He carried an illegal substance.

Driving dirty. Everyone does it, driving through life with the illegal substance of sin hiding in our hearts. We keep up appearances, but we still drive dirty, and it definitely dims the radiance in our lives.

Remember hearing, as a child, "Don't get your hands dirty! Don't get your dress dirty"? Now consumers have every kind of antibacterial soap the brand developers can dream up: scented, unscented, waterless, towelettes. But no one told us about driving dirty.

Jesus had an entirely different take on clean and unclean. Come along, and see.

miracles are not enough

In Matthew 14:15–36, the supernatural events happen faster than we can track them.

Jesus feeds five thousand men (plus miscellaneous wives and children) from a few measly loaves of bread and a couple of guppies,[1] then leaves that picnic and ships off the disciples in the boat.

Now Jesus heads to the mountainside to pray, then early in the morning walks over the water and the thrashing waves to greet the disciples who panic as they smash about in a storm at sea. Peter decides to give the walking-on-water thing a go, and off he strolls as well, right on top of the water, over those pitching waves. Only he forgets to keep his eyes on Jesus and sinks immediately, but still, what an adventure. Jesus grabs his hand, and they climb into the boat (normally a difficult task, if you're treading water and the boat is a foot higher than your head, but since Jesus is standing on top of the water, it's as easy as stepping over the side of your bathtub), and the storm immediately stops.

The boat heads for shore and Jesus and the disciples dock at Gennesaret, a place of great beauty, a fruitful plain on the northwest shore of the Sea of Galilee. People recognize Jesus, and word spreads of his team's arrival. But beauty is not enough for the masses. They want more. They've come for something from Jesus, not just a day of beauty. The sick stream toward Jesus from all the surrounding country and beg for healing, reaching out grasping hands in order to touch just the fringe of his robe. All who touch him are healed.

Meanwhile, back in the City of David, the Pharisees connive and conspire among themselves, wondering how to attack this popular holy man. They cast about in their narrow minds for inspiration, and then reach their huge "aha" moment. Tearing around the Sea of Galilee from Jerusalem all the way to this lovely area—some one hundred miles!—they throw down their gauntlet: "Why do your disciples break the tradition of the elders? They don't wash their hands before they eat!" (Matthew 15:2). Clearly they are very earnest. Controlling people usually are, and convincing, as well. They make great lawyers.

But this isn't about germs. No, they probably don't really understand germs and how germs and thus diseases transfer from person to person through our hands, our unwashed hands. The infectious disease specialists were a few years in coming. Rather, the Pharisees get so caught up in their rules, they stack them as high as Denver, to be sure they're squared away legally; these oral interpretations become the traditions of the Pharisees, with "wash your hands, your cups, your bowls, your spoons" only one segment of many (see Mark 7:3–4).

But God wants a relationship, and a relationship with God requires more than clean hands. God requires a clean heart. The Pharisees, on the other (clean) hand, just want to be right.

right versus relationship

I think about the Pharisees; in this account it's like they borrowed a stanza from the poem of my life. Like these Pharisees, I spend a great deal of time arguing over nonessentials, making sure that others understand me. Solomon got this too. Proverbs 18:2 reads,

"A fool finds no pleasure in understanding but delights in airing his own opinions." Ugh.

My energy and time would be better spent making sure I understand others, and caring less about their understanding of me. Because at least then I would be able to truly hear—and once we truly hear, we can begin to act as Christ's followers in this world, and our hearts and mouths begin to synchronize.

Too often we don't hear because we're so busy defending ourselves and accusing others; this can only be related to an unclean, damaged heart. At least, this is true for the way I live my life, my private life. My personal interactions with people who might inconvenience me take on the same defensive, accusing flavor— like the fish I bought once, a rare treat, fresh fish wrapped in lovely butcher paper, a long fish roll-up. I couldn't find the bundle and thought we'd left it at the grocery store on the conveyor belt. Days later, every time we got into our ancient green station wagon, the kids wrinkled their noses and projected gagging noises: "Argh. What's that smell?"

It took more than a month for me to place the two factors into the same equation. The lost fish was found in the back of the station wagon, a nice long roll of rotten fish.

That's me. That's my life. My interactions take on the rotten-fish scent of needing to be right. Then, if everyone agrees with me, we can have a relationship. Right versus relationship. This is how the Pharisees approached their rules and traditions too. They put so much focus on getting it right that they forgot the point of their clean rules—the relationship. And it's with this framework that they approach Jesus.

from miracle to minutia

Same song, second verse: how many times have I viewed life with this same framework? A child can be telling me a spectacular story from the day—a wondrous accounting of a hockey game or an interaction with a teacher or a real God encounter—and I will be distracted by the stain on the shirt, or the glass sweating on the antique table, or the chewing with an open mouth.

Once I called from a speaking engagement and became so upset in a conversation—probably a fine on an overdue video, something extremely worrisome and clearly worth harming relationships over—that I didn't take time to listen to good news my husband wanted to share. I shut him out with my anger. I found out several days later that his musical CD for children, *Room 4U & Me,* had won a Parents' Choice Approved Award—and I'd missed the miracle because I was caught up in another whirligig of worry and hand wringing and minutia.

So it is with the Pharisees.

The people are begging Jesus to just let them touch his cloak, the tassels on his robe; they're desperate and gathered round Jesus—and then up race the Pharisees, hot to trot about some trumped-up legal issue. They focus on the minutia and miss the miracle.

Realizing how far the Pharisees had to walk out on the plains to find Jesus and complain, I want to roll my eyes around in my head like a dashboard googly-eyed doll and shake the law-abiding zealots: "Do you have eyes to see? Do you have any idea what is going on around you? Do you know that people are being healed right and left, that the kingdom of God is in your midst? The lame walk, the blind see, Jesus raises the dead, and the hungry are fed! Don't you get it?"

No, they don't. The Pharisees want to know why the disciples didn't wash their hands before eating the miracle bread.

The rabble can't get enough of Jesus, and the rulers had their fill of him long before this moment. What a contrast. What a smoke screen. The Pharisees use word wars to defer attention. They know, deep down, that what they have is a passel of man-made rules that are supposed to keep them safe. They've been so busy trying to protect themselves from sin that they've built a wall of traditions that they just can't scale.

Jesus must be stricken by all the brokenness around him. He sees it in the crowds, in his disciples, and in the Pharisees and scribes.

Always before when reading this passage in Matthew 15, I heard an upset Jesus, shaking an angry fist at the Pharisees. Now, I also see his heartbreak. How he wants the people's hearts to be close to him. This is why he came.

Instead, the Pharisees nullify God's commandments with their elaborate interpretations. God says, "Honor your father and your mother," and the Pharisees say, "Good idea, except that I already promised to give my money to God. Too bad, so sad, sorry I can't help you, Mom and Dad."

Can it be—the Pharisees don't have to take care of their loved ones because they are all tied up with God? What a loss of all perspective when focusing on the rules rather than the One who made them.

Jesus aims his shotgun word: "Hypocrites!"

And they are—they are actors, putting on their piety when convenient, while inside, their hearts are not cleansed, not changed. Because changed hearts equal changed lives. When our hearts are close to God, our wrangling ceases, our words start to come out right, and our actions agree.

lip service

With their rules, the Pharisees play church, and all the while Jesus wants to offer so much more than commandments or letters chiseled on stone. Jesus hands the Pharisees the chance to live in the midst of the kingdom of God and not the letters of the Law, but the very Spirit!

"How much more glorious is the ministry that brings righteousness!" Paul exults, later, in 2 Corinthians 3:9. Righteousness. The very opposite of the Pharisees' hypocrisy.

How perfect that Jesus then quoted Isaiah 29:13 for the Pharisees:

> These people honor me with their lips, but their hearts are
> far from me. They worship me in vain; their teachings are
> but rules taught by men. (Matthew 15:8–9)

Isaiah knew about unclean lips (see Isaiah 6:1–8). After the death of King Uzziah, Isaiah was thrown into a vision where he saw the Lord seated high on a throne, the train of his robe filling the entire temple, surrounded by seraphs who called out:

Holy, holy, holy is the LORD Almighty;
  the whole earth is full of his glory.

The Scriptures tell us that "at the sound of their voices the doorposts and thresholds shook and the temple was filled with smoke."

Isaiah cried out, "Woe to me!... I am ruined! For I am a man of unclean lips, and I live among a people of unclean lips, and my eyes have seen the King, the LORD Almighty."

Isaiah knew of no remedy for his uncleanness, and then the seraph flew to the altar, clamped tongs around a burning coal, and touched the coal to Isaiah's mouth. "See, this has touched your lips; your guilt is taken away and your sin atoned for."

When Isaiah stood in the presence of God, he knew the guilt in his heart and how it showed up on his mouth. He knew that his lips were unclean.

Oh, to have a heart like Isaiah's that immediately wails, "I am ruined! I am undone!"—a heart convicted with the truth that we too are unclean.

Think about Isaiah's mouth—figuratively speaking, his lips would never be the same. If the seraph burned his lips with the fiery coal, then forever after, every word from Isaiah's mouth would breathe past those scars. Every fluff of air, every unkind syllable, every poorly expressed desire would catch on the wounds around his lips. I can only imagine the impact on Isaiah as a prophet, as a speaker, as a representative of God in the world: he would be aware of every sentence, using each one wisely, knowing the cost of uncleanness. Every word he uttered would be singed from God's presence, from being forgiven and cleansed and touched by the burning coals of holiness.

it's not about your hands

Think again on that moment that Jesus quotes Isaiah and then calls the crowd closer. Imagine being beckoned by Jesus in such a way, being set free and made clean by the gift he's brought, because here are freedom and grace.

"Listen and understand," Jesus says. "What goes into a man's mouth does not make him 'unclean,' but what comes out of his mouth, that is what makes him 'unclean'" (Matthew 15:10–11).

Surely the crowd heaves a huge sigh. The people's anxiety eats a hole in their pockets of faith. All these rules! How can they possibly keep them all straight, let alone obey even a fraction of them? To this hopeless group with the rule phobia, certain of never getting things right, Jesus's words must sound like freedom. *So it's not about what you eat?* these rule keepers must think. *It's not about whether you washed your hands or not? Hallelujah!*

the faraway heart

Later, to his disciples, Jesus clarifies the unclean process: "The things that come out of the mouth come from the heart, and these make a man 'unclean.' For out of the heart come evil thoughts, murder, adultery, sexual immorality, theft, false testimony, slander. These are what make a man 'unclean'; but eating with unwashed hands does not make him 'unclean'" (verses 18–20).

In the movie *As Good as It Gets,* Jack Nicholson plays novelist Melvin Udall, who obsessively washes his hands, refuses to touch silverware in restaurants, and can hardly get out the door because of his paralysis about germs. Melvin's hands are clean and his germ-code pristine, but his heart is so riddled with fear, prejudice, anger, and lack of love that his language and actions spew out like a polluted stream.

The freedom offered to the Melvins of this world, and to us, the great gift from Jesus, is the gift of heart cleanness. Maybe we try to keep our hands free from sin, but sin starts in the heart; it nestles in there like a lizard curled on a hot rock, and then slithers its way out through our words and into our actions. The Pharisees got it backward, and so do we.

"Each one is tempted when," James said (1:14–15), "by his own evil desire, he is dragged away and enticed. Then, after desire has conceived, it gives birth to sin; and sin, when it is full-grown, gives birth to death."

The Pharisees give birth to death with all their backward rules, and miss the gift of a clean heart.

This explains Jesus's heartbreak when he talks to them, the depth of his frustration because they so totally miss the point. They are sharpening the wrong pencil, focusing on their rules when Jesus says, "No more lip service! Let's start with a clean heart! I'll wash you, then you'll be clean. Then your lips will agree with your heart and your actions will follow suit." And then the words from Isaiah 29:13, "These people honor me with their lips, but their hearts are far from me," will no longer apply to us, to the church in general, which suffers daily and chronically from the need of a bath, a cleansing that reaches beyond the antibacterial gel that we carry in our purses.

the rabble and the rule keepers

So imagine, then, Jesus in the middle of all these people who lip-sync holiness. (Scrub your hands! Wash those pots! Clean the kettle! Don't touch that! Don't eat that! You can't sit there!) Jesus knows true holiness—he *is* true holiness and will be crucified for our uncleanness, that we might finally, at last, be declared holy and clean. Jesus stands there with the rule keepers and the rabble. The rabble want only to touch him so that they can be healed; the rule keepers want to use their words to make others look bad and themselves look good.

What longing must rise up in Jesus's heart for them to truly see, understand, and know the enormity of their sin and the gift before them. The fulfillment of all those rules, right in their presence, and they can only see the rules.

How much Jesus wants them to just examine their own hearts, the right response to being in the presence of holiness.

I get that. Being around people with pure lips highlights our own sin and motivates us to self-examination. When I return from a meeting with my covenant group, or my critique group, or have spent time with other radiant friends and watched their thoughtful ways and listened to their wise words and tactful loving, I'm challenged. These are holy women, who keep short lists, repent quickly, invite God (and their friends) to probe for sin and to help them grow. They are so like Jesus, and they make me want to be like Jesus too.

I think Isaiah learned to respond through his encounter with God in the vision he describes in chapter 6. He learned to listen, turned his ear to God, and was undone by God's holiness. He learned to repent early in his tenure as a prophet. In the presence of God's holiness—and the train that filled the temple is a picture of the immensity of God's holiness—Isaiah found his own sinfulness and moved immediately to God. Finally, the prophet learned, through singed lips, to heed God's calling. His response was immediate: "Here am I. Send me!" (verse 8).

Our personality fractures when there's a breach between our lips and our hearts. We become schizophrenic believers, two different people inside one body, and Jesus stands in the midst of that breach, the Word that brings life and holiness, and invites us to bring our lips and our hearts together through him (see Matthew 15:8). Jesus longs for wholeness for us, a oneness, the root meaning of *integrity.*

It all begins with cleanness.

a new kind of clean

Jesus offers a different kind of cleansing, like spring cleaning instead of a hurried dusting on Wednesday afternoon before Grandmother arrives. As David pleaded, "Wash away all my iniquity and cleanse me from my sin" (Psalm 51:2), Jesus offers the cleansing flow of forgiveness, an entirely new start for our old hearts.

Don't we need this desperately?

Paul says in Ephesians 5:25–26, "Christ loved the church and gave himself up for her to make her holy, cleansing her by the washing with water through the word." Christ *gave himself up* for us, washing us with himself, with his purity, his sinless life, that we might be fully cleansed.

In the letter to Titus, Paul reiterates this beautifully: "But when the kindness and love of God our Savior appeared, he saved us, not because of righteous things we had done, but because of his mercy. He saved us through the washing of rebirth and renewal by the Holy Spirit, whom he poured out on us generously through Jesus Christ our Savior" (3:4–6).

Because of God's kindness, love, mercy—not because we wash our hands!—God saves us. Through Jesus Christ our Savior—washing of rebirth! Renewal by the Holy Spirit. This is what Jesus offers the Pharisees, offers the disciples, offers us. No salt scrub or seaweed bath required, fun though that might be, radiant though that might make us. No, our radiance comes from being so well washed by Christ, we're like brilliant white laundry hanging on the line in the sunshine.

When I heard the story of the young man "driving dirty," I thought, *How much easier to just drive clean. Then you don't have to worry about being pulled over and searched.* Imagine the freedom to relax by giving God permission to search our cars, to look through our hearts, sift through the rubble and rebellion, look under the seats of our souls and the consoles of our conscience—because then we can drive clean. What peace and assurance then.

No matter what happens, nothing is buried in our hearts. No debris, no illegal substances, none of the stuff Jesus said makes us unclean. Like the saying "Cleanliness is next to godliness," maybe that's what radiance means, after all.

come along to...

 • transfer from dark to light •

Dear God—
That's a really long list.
You know the thoughts I have that are less than good.
Far less, frankly.
You know the times I have stolen someone's reputation
Through doubt or storytelling.
You know the times I've hated,
And you call it murder.
You know all about my
Faraway heart.
Please, Lord.
Please forgive me.
Please cleanse the inside of my soul
So that all the words that come from me ring pure.
Help me to experience true forgiveness
And learn to live in that
Fresh-washed
State.

• transfix upon Christ •

As you are still before God, what shows up in your heart? Ask the Lord to help you experience true forgiveness, and then wait there until you do. Let your repentance turn to praise as you rejoice in a clean heart.

• translate the meaning •

- With whom do you most relate, the rule keepers or the rabble? Why? How do you see that in yourself?
- How does the faraway heart show up for you? What impact does it have on your relationships? Invite God to do a clean sweep of your soul as you create your list.
- Describe one of your "Woe is me—I am undone!" times.
- Which phases of Isaiah's cycle trouble you? Learning to listen, to repent, to respond? When has repentance solidified into true change? When has it opened up a new calling for you, as it did for Isaiah?
- When have you experienced the just-washed cleansing of Christ? How does that affect your relationships?

• transform by renewing your mind •

Let us draw near to God with a sincere heart in full assurance of faith, having our hearts sprinkled to cleanse us from a guilty conscience and having our bodies washed with pure water.

Hebrews 10:22

• transparency through prayer •

Dear God,
I do not live in a place of beauty
Because of the choices I make,
And yet you call me to you.
You invite me to be healed.
You bring the coal and you singe my lips
And you purify my heart.
Help me, Lord, to live with
My heart so close to you
That my words and my actions
Seem more and more
Like words you would say
And things you would do.
So I reach out my hand
And touch the veil of your holiness
And I know
You are present in my life.
Make a difference, Lord,
Through me.
In Jesus's name,
Amen.

• transpired action •

How will you let God cleanse your heart today?

come along
to the garden

Illuminations on Becoming Yourself

"Greetings.... Do not be afraid."
—MATTHEW 28:9–10

Not only does Christ say to you that your heart
is good, he invites you now out of the shadows
to unveil your glory.... God endowed you with
a glory when he created you, a glory so deep and
mythic that all creation pales in comparison....
The deeper reason that we fear our own glory is
that once we let others see it, they will have seen
the truest us, and that is nakedness indeed.
We can repent of our sin. We can work on our
"issues." But there is nothing to be "done"
about our glory. It's so naked. It's just there—the
truest us. It is an awkward thing to shimmer
when everyone else around you is not, to walk

in your glory with an unveiled face
when everyone else is veiling his.
—JOHN ELDREDGE

I hadn't seen her in years, other than a glimpse here and there, a hurried hello in the halls at school or perhaps the grocery store. She'd had family problems, and the wear and tear drained the light from her face as though someone had thrown the switch, turned off the electricity. She looked the picture of despondency and depression, as though dying minute by minute.

So when I saw her in the lobby of the theater, I barely recognized her. She practically shimmered. She looked like she'd been on a television makeover show, where they spend millions of dollars flying in experts to rebuild you from the teeth outward... except she was the same height, weight, even with the same hair color. Only now she dressed stylishly, in colors and styles that graced her, but this was a tribute to being free from depression's dull grasp.

I stumbled around for words, not wanting her to feel as though she'd looked like the hinges on death's door in the past. "You are glowing! Tell me what is going on in your life!"

Her smile lit up the lobby. "I've had some real breakthroughs in counseling and have finally really discovered how much Jesus really loves me."

That sounds trite until you see her. She could put the spas out of business with that kind of testimonial.

real radiance

Flip the pages of magazines, stroll the department store cosmetics counters, tour your local drugstore makeup aisle, and you will see entire product lines dedicated to the principle of radiance, all intent on making us look younger and naturally glowing. Tanning sprays, lotions, foundation, eye shadow: all to create the appearance of sheen and a quality applied externally.

But true radiance, like my friend displays, does not come with application instructions like a box of hair dye. True radiance is as Charles Wesley described in the hymn "Love Divine, All Loves Excelling":

> Finish, then, thy new creation;
> pure and spotless let us be.
> Let us see thy great salvation
> perfectly restored in thee;
> changed from glory into glory,
> till in heaven we take our place,
> till we cast our crowns before thee,
> lost in wonder, love, and praise.

True radiance requires a reflective quality, and the women I know who glow are not shallow crowd followers but insightful, deep, reflective people. They sort through all the data flying at them: the hardship, the disappointment, the loss, the heartache, their own sin, and the good stuff as well. They riffle through the data and decide what they will let in, what they will allow to impact them. They choose to respond positively to potentially negative events by moving straight back to God. Maybe they even reflect it back to God from the mirror of their souls, so that God absorbs it.

Looking at these radiant women is like examining a cache of diamonds to understand their sparkle. The charcoal of their past, the pressures of their lives, all exerted such force upon their souls that they do what diamonds do: they shine, sparkle, radiate brilliance when the Son catches the facets of their hearts.

Just so, the two radiant women at the tomb, for whom the pressures of their past created a depth and brilliance after another dazzling encounter with the Light of the World. Come along to the garden. Come along and see how, once again, the Son lights the way for us.

a new day

The women have lived through their lives' greatest heartbreak in the past three days. Their Messiah, their leader and Lord, ended up on a cross rather than a throne, and as they swiped at their tears and swallowed their grief, they wrapped his body for burial.

Now, the day after Passover, they return to the garden to visit Jesus's tomb.

"How will we roll away the stone?" one of them asks. A huge rock seals the mouth of the tomb, and guards await them at the grave. The women's hearts heave with regret, the regret of loss, inadequacy, and the sharp pain of disappointment in themselves, but also in this man they trusted to lead them into a new future.

Suddenly, the ground reverberates as an earthquake shakes itself free, as though groaning, echoing the women's heaving hearts. And there, rolling away and then sitting on the stone, is an angel of the Lord, looking like lightning, with garments as radiant as fresh-fallen snow.

The guards watch the stone rolling away and the angel descending. Panic seizes them. They shake and become like dead men, passing out stone cold on the ground outside the tomb.

Though no words have been exchanged, the angel answers the women, "Do not be afraid, for I know that you are looking for Jesus, who was crucified. He is not here; he has risen, just as he said."

Mary Magdalene and the other Mary don't know whether to laugh or scream or cry some more. The stone rolls away, and the guards pass out. Now an angel talks to them? They did not expect to find the tomb empty. They've returned to give Jesus a proper burial, and now Jesus isn't here? Maybe the angel made a mistake.

Before they can respond, the angel again answers, "Come and see the place where he lay."

They peer into the tomb, spotting the burial strips, with the head covering lying separately. But no Jesus. Not here? He is risen? What does the angel mean?

The angel hustles them through their regret and silent questions. "Hurry! Run now! Tell the others to go quickly into Galilee, where they will see him."

The women rush away, the angel-words ringing in their ears,

their hearts beating with fear as they run, with joy keeping pace in this race to spread the news (see Matthew 28:1–8).

do not be afraid

Mary Magdalene knows fear. Christ delivered her from seven demons, and she well remembers the absolute terror of those days. But now, as she dashes from the garden tomb, a different fear pounds in her ears: fear of the unknown and the not understood, fear of the emptiness at the tomb and within her own heart. Who are they, without Jesus? How do they live? They have lost all they believed in, and lost their identities in the process. So engrossed are they in their thoughts and the surprising morning that she and Mary run headlong into Jesus.

"Greetings." What a perfect understatement!

When they see who is speaking, joy lights their faces and battles with the fear. Surely wonder covers them like the early-morning dew. The women fall to their knees and clasp his feet, bowing low in worship. They do not understand, but they can't *not* worship.

Then Jesus says, "Do not be afraid."

Do not be afraid? Do not be afraid! This time the words sink into their souls and the joy replaces the fear, filters in like sunrise replaces the night.

Just like that turn from night to day, replacing fear is a process, but our rules have helped us control our fear so well. Fear comes naturally when we renounce our rules for managing the universe, others, and ourselves, when we relinquish the unspoken rules, the token rules.

As we let go, we draw breathtakingly nearer to the one who longs for relationship over rules, who longs for us rather than an outward compliance with the endless list of letters written in stone.

Oh, to toss aside our rules of order and run to Jesus, the one who met Mary and Mary in the garden and said, with such thoughtfulness and kindness, "Do not be afraid."

Jesus's words echo his mountain hike with Peter, James, and John.

There, looking up at Jesus, the disciples fell facedown in fear and worship, because his being was transfigured into a whiteness beyond any bleach on earth. And then, when God split apart the heavens yet again, saying, "This is my beloved Son; listen to him," Jesus stepped forward.

He reached over and told Peter, James, and John, "Arise. And do not be afraid" (see Matthew 17:1–7). "Do not be afraid. Do not be afraid." Jesus has words for us about our fear. Listen to him, God says. Listen!

It is the fear that immobilizes us, the fear that hardens our hold on the familiar. We know the rules; we know them and can't release them, though their usefulness has long disappeared. Though they hurt us more than they help us manage, or better yet grow through, life.

Fear wraps itself around us like the tendrils from a grapevine, a kudzulike stranglehold fear of displeasing others when we want so badly to be loved, accepted. Fear that we can't extricate ourselves from following everyone's guidelines, that we will never make the next cut in the contest called life.

becoming ourselves

It all comes down to one fear, doesn't it? One insecurity lies at the bottom of all these rules. Somehow, someone or many people communicated that their comfort depends on your compliance: *You must be like me, like I think you need to be, or else my own world crumbles and my own fragile grasp on life disintegrates with it. My world is more manageable if you think like I think, act like I act, and live like I live.*

But even that isn't really the bottom. Beneath all our rules is the basic fear that we're not enough, that being ourselves isn't good enough. And when this fear veils our faces, we live behind the curtain. This fear is the truth. We're *not* good enough. We can't comply with all the rules and layers of expectations, any more than the lay Israelites could, or the Pharisees.

Becoming ourselves is an uncharted path. When Mary and Mary run from the tomb, they run into a life they've never known before. No one can help them discover who they will be with Christ no longer beside them to teach them. But now they will have a Tutor, because in a matter of days Jesus will leave the Holy Spirit with them to lead them, teach them, convict them of sin, and invite them into the next step of their path.

No one has ever been like you before, so you can't follow anyone else's example. No map contains the little red dots that mark off your trail. This is an uncharted path that only you can travel. All we know for sure is that, as it says on the map, "You Are Here."

Fear, then, accosts us in the tomb, just before dawn, just before the angel rolls away the stone.

But listen.

Do you feel the rumbling? The guards at the tomb of your life shake and become like dead men. Let go the old guard, the rules you've lived by, taught by, and labored beneath. The letter of the law has expired. You can let the stone roll out of the mouth of the cave and into this new day, new life, new you. Lean into Jesus, the one who meets you at the tomb that has become your life. He waits for you and invites you, just as he invited Mary Magdalene and Mary.

"Do not be afraid, but go…"

In breathtaking radiance, you can go into this world like a new bride, clothed in the white of forgiveness, the brilliance of vulnerability, the hope and healing of the life you're living in Christ. You can become…yourself, the person Christ calls you to be, the woman God imagined you to be all along, and—more good news—you do not have to go alone.

feast of Pentecost

Fifty days after Mary and Mary's garden encounter, the people gather for the Feast of Pentecost.[1]

This celebration came to represent the giving of the Law, when Moses climbed Mount Sinai to meet with God, then climbed back down clutching the two stone tablets. The Law highlighting our total inability to meet its demands, the Law directing us to the one who could and would fulfill all its demands.

Suddenly, into the midst of the festival celebrating the Law, the breath of God blows in the form of the Holy Spirit, alighting on the new believers, setting fire to the new church, and replacing the glorious letter of the law with a far-surpassing radiance. At the Feast of Pentecost, God exchanged the law written in stone for the law written on our hearts. He replaced the deadly letter of the law with the Spirit that gives life (see 2 Corinthians 3:6).

And now, long after Moses, the glory of God shows up on the people of God—on your face, on my face—and no veil dims that radiance. There's no need to cover up or pretend any longer.

Such a dramatic moment, and yet somehow most of us have missed it. We spend so much of our lives trying to fit in, between all our rules and worrying about how we don't measure up—worrying how we're built differently than our best girlfriend or how we inherited the family hips or the height or the nose. But what matters isn't about how tall or short, thin or wide, flat or round we are—it's about how God fills the space that is you, and how you fill your space in this world.

A wooden sign hangs next to my daughter's mirror, painted with a bright goopy grinning sun and the words scrawled like a child's hand:

> God is watching you
> because he loves you so much
> and he can't keep his eyes off you!

Oh, that we would catch his gaze and live in that love. So long ago, God said to Solomon, "I have chosen and consecrated this temple so that my Name may be there forever. My eyes and my heart will always be there" (2 Chronicles 7:16).

And now, we are the temple where God lives. We are the portable sanctuary that houses the Lord Jesus. God's eyes and heart and now Spirit will always be with us. So what is there to fear? Nothing! The Scriptures tell us that Jesus "is the radiance of [God's] glory and the exact representation of His nature, and upholds all things by the word of His power" (Hebrews 1:3, NASB).

a new reflection

Hear that? This is good news! You don't rush out of the tomb on self-directed batteries. You're upheld this very minute by the word of Christ's power, by Christ's powerful word. Christ the Word upholds you by his word. Can it get better than this?

Yes, even better. As we relinquish all those rules, as we spend time with Christ, our countenance changes.

The old adage says that the more time you spend with a person, the more you look alike. Haven't we seen married people who, after fifty years, look like they could be fraternal twins? We've also seen people who, frighteningly enough, resemble their dogs.

Isn't it glorious, then, this invitation to become more and more like Jesus? "And we, who with unveiled faces all reflect the Lord's glory, are being transformed into his likeness with ever-increasing glory, which comes from the Lord, who is the Spirit" (2 Corinthians 3:18).

Day after day, you look in the mirror and just see yourself: same hair, laugh lines, smile, eyes. Same bags and sags too, but try not to look at those. What if, each day, you pray, "Lord Jesus, let me look like you to those I meet today"? And then one day, you look in the mirror, and you see Jesus there too.

Maybe it works a little like this: Remember those wooden images at amusement parks, maybe Mickey and Minnie Mouse, only all you see is their painted bodies and a cutout where their faces would be? You jump behind the board and peer out of the face hole. Of course it doesn't match, no one is fooled, but it provides a silly picture for you to cram into a drawer.

Instead of these cartoon characters, here on earth we are the bodies, and we step behind Jesus's face, so that when people look at us, they see him. They will see Jesus's face, his eyes looking out of our eyes; his love, his words pouring out of our mouths; his hands, working through us; his might, powering us.

And when we look at others, we see Jesus too, finding the God print within each person we encounter. Knowing that God formed them and then called us to help lead them to Jesus.

dribbling sunshine

Steam rises off my coffee, like a smoke signal of peace. The water of the lake sparkles radiantly, and just *is*—just there, being a lake, letting the sun do what it will do, reflect off a reflecting surface.

Maybe that is our answer: shining isn't something we *do*. Shining happens when we let the sun—rather, the Son—do what he does. The Son is brilliant, bright, filled with glory, radiant with God; and when the Son shines, if we are Son bathing, then we too reflect that glory. We too will be radiant with God's presence.

Like the sunflower on my table: tall, stately, absolutely stunning; like the sun on a stick, dribbling gold dust that puddles on its leaves and pools up on the table at its base.

Come along to...

 • transfer from dark to light •

Dear God!
I've lived too long in the tomb
And now you've rolled away
That stone and positioned an angel
At the mouth.
"Don't be afraid,"
you say,
but I have been afraid,
very afraid.
Forgive me for my tomblike living,
For my fear,
For my face that bears no
Resemblance to Jesus whatsoever.
And with your forgiveness,
Lord,
Bring your light,
Bring your salvation,
Bring your radiance,
That I might reflect
Your glory
Today.
And tomorrow.

• transfix upon Christ •

Enter into stillness with some deep breaths. Settle your soul by praying, "Come, Lord Jesus." And then be silent. Just rest there, held by God, loved by God.

• translate the meaning •

- How many people do you know who are truly radiant? What are some of their characteristics that you admire? When do you feel radiant?
- Talk about the role of fear in your life. Where and when do you feel fear? How do you handle it? Which rules are hardest to relinquish? Why?
- What scares you about becoming yourself?
- In what ways do you long to be more like Jesus? Where do you see Christ in you? Where is transformation visible?
- How will you invite others to become their best selves through Christ?
- Who are the guards at the mouth of the tomb, the people who do not want you to live in the fullness that Jesus offers, in the life and hope that he brings? How can you move into the good news that the Law has been fulfilled and you are free to live life in the Spirit, with the glorious radiance of a woman deeply loved and deeply forgiven?

• transform by renewing your mind •

Now to Him who is able to do exceedingly abundantly above all that we ask or think, according to the power that works in us, to Him be glory in the church by Christ Jesus to all generations, forever and ever. Amen.

Ephesians 3:20–21, NKJV

And we, who with unveiled faces all reflect the Lord's glory, are being transformed into his likeness with ever-increasing glory, which comes from the Lord, who is the Spirit.

2 Corinthians 3:18

• transparency through prayer •

Yes, God!
I bow in worship,
throw myself at your feet,
and then heed your kind touch.
"Arise. And do not be afraid."
And I rise
And move through the damp grass
And into this new day
Loved,
Forgiven,
Empowered,
Upheld

By your powerful
Word.
Allow me,
Dear God,
To become myself as you
See me
And to be part of your plan
For breathing life
Into your people.
Into this world.
Amen.

• transpired action •

How will you "become you" today?

The Girlfriends' Guide to *Come Along*

How to use this book in group discussion

When I think of Jesus, and indeed read the Scriptures, I see him often in community, challenging others, laughing with them, loving them both individually and as a group. *Come Along* is designed to easily facilitate just such camaraderie with Jesus and with others. Isolation is one of the enemies of spiritual growth, and when we gather in common need and even common dysfunction, our hearts begin to break open. Sharing deeply from our souls is a learned process that gets easier the more we practice, the more we wait together, the more we learn to love and accept.

Consider whom God might long to gather together into a small group. Maybe they are neighbors, or parents from school, or women you've seen in the mothers' group, at the bus stop, on the commuter train to work. Perhaps they line the pews with you, beautiful but their silence masking a deep longing for friends, for a Jesus who is real in the midst of real problems and real pain. Pray and invite some women into community, to break through the isolation so deadly in our world today.

And then *Come Along,* companions on a journey guaranteed to stitch your lives together in a fabric shimmering with radiance and life, like gold lamé.

Some basic group guidelines:

1. **Make certain the group understands** this pivotal rule: what is shared here, stays here. Stories shared in your group are not for broadcast, public dissection, debate with friends, or posting on the prayer chain—they are for your ears only, and not to be repeated. This agreement creates safety and the ability to be vulnerable.

2. **Listen to one another** with genuine openness. Don't judge, blame, try to fix problems, or silence someone's tears. Don't be afraid of those tears or feel as though you must have the wisdom of a counselor or therapist in order to hear another's stories and pain. The Holy Spirit can be the counselor, and you can be the arms of Jesus around one another. You need no answers. You just need to love, and be loved by one another through Christ.

3. **Remember that going deep with others takes time,** but that it is worth the wait, and the discomfort, and even the embarrassment of sharing your soul's secrets.

4. **Keep in contact** if possible throughout the week. When we share deeply, telling stories that perhaps have never seen the light of day, shame sneaks in quickly when we are alone again.

5. **Finally, keep it simple.** You don't need to have a bunch of snacks, thirteen types of beverages, and a gorgeous and clean home in which to meet. You just need to be together. A pitcher of water and some glasses do just fine. Besides, you may need to rehydrate as you come face to face with Jesus through one another and tears leak through your reserve.

when you meet...

Decide the structure for your group gatherings. A five- or ten-week commitment may be just perfect, with a couple of snow days (or hurricane days, depending on your locale!) or interruption days built in for wiggle room.

As your group's personality forms, pick and choose the elements you'll highlight based on the length of your time together. Don't be afraid to invite women out of their comfort zones as doubts surface, such as, "We've never done this before," or, "We've never prayed aloud together," or, "We've never waited in silence"—and remind your group that when we stretch, we grow. I think Jesus must beam at us when we move toward him in new ways, like a loving parent reaching out to grab the hands of a just-toddling toddler.

gathering

Open with a prayer. Even, "Come, Lord Jesus," said by one person, then echoed by the group in unison, works wonderfully.

Read aloud together some opening words of Jesus, perhaps the illuminating encounter-with-Jesus passage near the start of each chapter in this book.

group discussion

This can be informal. No lecture style is necessary. Ask one another:
- What spoke to you from this first section?
- What did you highlight and why?
- What feelings showed up for you? Fear, anger, pain, shame? What is behind that? What can you say about that?

- Where were there tears or the "aha" moments?
- How did you feel about the personal encounter with Jesus, as shared in the Scripture story?
- Where do you have questions?

application

The closing section of each chapter provides a variety of ways to interact in your group as well as individually with the ideas of *Come Along*. Pick and choose, change it up weekly if you like, but don't overlook the powerful bonding that occurs as you move with others into applying to everyday life what you're learning about God, Jesus, the Holy Spirit, and faith in them. Come along, then, to…

transfer from dark to light — Consider praying aloud as a group this confession, this place of repentance. Confession is good for the soul and begins a deep mending of both the individual and of the fabric of community.

transfix upon Christ — Though initially uncomfortable, silence is a powerful tool in a group. Invite the women into stillness and just wait. Someone can be in charge of the clock. Try this for two minutes, then stretch into five. Gently invite the women back into the world of words, and ask, "How did you experience God in that silence? What was hard? What might Christ be pressing on your heart?"

translate the meaning — This is the stuff of discussion. Guide this time softly, but try to keep the women on track. Invite them into reflection as you read the questions out loud.

Don't worry if it takes a minute for answers to formulate and be voiced. Give folks the space to be comfortable with digging deeper in the group setting. Remember, there's no right or wrong answer to these questions. The hope is that together we will process, share our experiences and fears and joy, and come alongside one another in this never-ending journey with Jesus.

transform by renewing your mind — Try reading this Scripture aloud together, or back and forth from one half of the group to the other. Perhaps you will want to memorize the Scriptures as a group and share them the following week. Maybe hand out three-by-five cards so each woman can write out the passage and hold on to it in during the next days. Ask: how does this passage apply to me; what might God be inviting me to do here, or speaking to my soul about?

transparency through prayer — Again, a place of honest prayer. Read aloud, or read it silently, or have just one person read it. Put yourself in the middle of that prayer.

transpired action — Ask each other, perhaps in groups of two: how will you come along today, based on this story?

closing

Close the time together in prayer, inviting God to plant the words from Jesus into the soil of your soul.

Acknowledgments

To name all the people influencing my life at such critical junctures would be overwhelming, for me, and for you. Without my Critique Group (Lynn Austin, Joy Bocanegra, Cleo Lampos) I would still be worrying with my first article rather than finishing my eleventh book. My Covenant Group (Adele Calhoun, Karen Mains, Linda Richardson, Marilyn Stewart, Sibyl Towner) sends up flares for me to light the dark path.

Writer-speaker friends and mentors Lin Johnson, Tish Suk, the amazing women of Advanced Writers and Speakers Association, and Carol Kent understand my life and have prayed me daily through the corridors.

My extended family—Jack and Shirley Henderson and Jim and Marie Rubietta; my brother and sister, John Henderson and Sara Kelley—mean the world to me and keep loving me even when I am buried under piles of words. And my family—Rich, Ruthie, Zak, and Josh: You exemplify for me the Light of the World. You make me want to be transformed, from glory to glory. Thank you.

And may the Light of the World be pleased to illuminate the path, a few steps ahead, for us all through his presence in *Come Along*.

Notes

Chapter 1: Come Along to the River

The epigraph to this chapter is drawn from Richard A. Swenson, MD, *Margin: Restoring Emotional, Physical, Financial, and Time Reserves to Overloaded Lives* (Colorado Springs: NavPress, 1992), 30.

1. Kaufmann Kohler and Isaac Broydé, "Commandments, the 613," JewishEncyclopedia.com, www.jewishencyclopedia .com/view.jsp?artid=689&letter=C, accessed 30 July 2008.

2. "Foot Binding," http://en.wikipedia.org/wiki/Foot_binding, accessed 30 July 2008.

Chapter 2: Come Along to the Temple

The epigraph to this chapter is drawn from Paul Tournier, as quoted in William P. Young, *The Shack* (Newbury Park, CA: Windblown Media, 2007), 18.

1. With thanks to Nancy Groom, author of *From Bondage to Bonding: Escaping Codependency; Embracing Biblical Love* (Colorado Springs: NavPress, 1991) and *Risking Intimacy: Overcoming Fear, Finding Rest* (Grand Rapids, MI: Baker, 2000), who years ago began talking with me about women wearing white.

Chapter 3: Come Along to the Parade

The epigraph to this chapter is drawn from Augustine, as quoted in David G. Benner, *The Gift of Being Yourself: The Sacred Call to Self-Discovery* (Downers Grove, IL: InterVarsity, 2004), 20.

1. Edward W. Goodrick and John R. Kohlenberger III, *Zondervan NIV Exhaustive Concordance* (Grand Rapids, MI: Zondervan, 1999), 1597, s.v. Greek word number 5505.

Chapter 4: Come Along to the Courtroom

The epigraph to this chapter is drawn from Frederick Buechner, *Listening to Your Life* (New York: HarperCollins, 1992), 132.

1. Luke 18:4–5; author's paraphrase of verses 1–3 preceding.
2. George Arthur Buttrick, ed., *The Interpreter's Bible,* 12 vols. (Nashville: Abingdon-Cokesbury, 1951–57), 8:307.
3. "Under Old Testament law, judges were to fear God (i.e., consider that he will judge those who break his law and mistreat others) and therefore defend the oppressed. Many ancient societies had severe legal penalties for unjust judges." Craig S. Keener, *The IVP Bible Background Commentary: New Testament* (Downers Grove, IL: InterVarsity, 1994), 238.

Chapter 5: Come Along to the Crowd

1. *When a Man Loves a Woman,* directed by Luis Mandok (1994; Burbank, CA: Buena Vista Pictures).
2. Author's paraphrase. See parallel gospel accounts in Matthew 9:20–22 and Mark 5:25–34.

3. Author's paraphrase of Matthew 9:20–22; Mark 5:25–34; Luke 8:43–48.

4. Francine Rivers, *The Last Sin Eater* (Wheaton, IL: Tyndale, 1998), 259–60.

Chapter 6: Come Along to the Party

The epigraph to this chapter is drawn from Thomas C. Oden, ed., *The Ancient Christian Devotional: A Year of Weekly Readings* (Downers Grove, IL: InterVarsity, 2007), 198.

1. Edward W. Goodrick and John R. Kohlenberger III, *Zondervan NIV Exhaustive Concordance* (Grand Rapids, MI: Zondervan, 1999), 1590, s.v. Greek word number 4981.

2. Craig S. Keener, *The IVP Bible Background Commentary: New Testament* (Downers Grove, IL: InterVarsity, 1994), 209.

3. Keener, *IVP Bible Background Commentary,* 209.

Chapter 7: Come Along to the Meadow

The epigraph to this chapter is drawn from *The Pillar of Cloud* (1833), "Lead Kindly Light," stanza 1, by John Henry Cardinal Newman.

1. Gerald May, as quoted in Anne Lamott, *Plan B: Further Thoughts on Faith* (New York: Riverhead, 2005), 233.

2. George Arthur Buttrick, ed., *The Interpreter's Bible,* 12 vols. (Nashville: Abingdon-Cokesbury, 1951–57), 12:106.

3. Craig S. Keener, *The IVP Bible Background Commentary: New Testament* (Downers Grove, IL: InterVarsity, 1994), 712.

Chapter 8: Come Along to the Synagogue

The epigraph to this chapter is drawn from Clement of Alexandria, *The Westminster Collection of Christian Quotations*, ed. Martin H. Manser (Louisville, KY: Westminster John Knox, 2001), 177, quoted in Kathleen Long Bostrom, *Finding Calm in the Chaos* (Louisville, KY: Westminster John Knox, 2006), 138.

Chapter 9: Come Along to the Plains

The epigraph to this chapter is drawn from C. S. Lewis, *Mere Christianity* (New York: Macmillan, 1960), 64.

1. The Scriptures actually tell us "five loaves of bread and two fish," but evidently in the original language these are about the size of a hard little roll a child might put in his lunch, and what are two fish compared to the size of the crowd? Pretty small.

Chapter 10: Come Along to the Garden

The epigraph to this chapter is drawn from John Eldredge, *Waking the Dead* (Nashville: Thomas Nelson, 2003), 73, 78, 87.

1. "Pentecost or Shavuot Overview," biblicalholidays.com, http://biblicalholidays.com/Pentecost/pentecost-overview .htm, accessed 1 August 2008.

About the Author

Jane Rubietta is known for her vulnerability, spiritual depth, and humor as a popular and riveting keynote speaker. She speaks internationally and is the author of eleven books, including the critically acclaimed *Come Closer* and the award-winning *Grace Points* and *Quiet Places*.

She and her husband, Rich, founded the nonprofit Abounding Ministries with the mission of offering a life-changing experience of God's love in Christ Jesus through music, writing, speaking, and retreats for communities, schools, and churches.

After obtaining her bachelor of science degree from Indiana University School of Business, Jane completed postgraduate studies in Germany while also directing an international drama team, taking the gospel into then-communist countries. She worked on her master's degree at Trinity Divinity School in Deerfield, Illinois.

Between writing and speaking engagements, Jane serves as assistant coordinator of the Write-to-Publish writers conference (www.writetopublish.com). She belongs to Speak Up Speaker Services and the Advanced Writers and Speakers Association. Jane and her husband, a pastor and award-winning composer, live in Illinois and have three children.

For more information, or to consider Jane to speak at your women's event, retreat, conference, convention, or training seminars, or to learn more about Abounding Ministries, visit Jane online at www.JaneRubietta.com.

Come Closer
— to life, Jesus, and a new you.

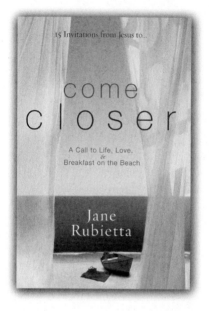

With humor, unforgettable experiences, and encouragement, *Come Closer* features questions for Bible Study and discussion, plus application exercises, leading readers into a richer spiritual life that feasts on Heaven's promises.